CONSTABLE

This guide book contains exact bu[t] explore the borderlands of Suffolk an[d] Country and the valley of the lovely [Stour ... ... planned our] routes in such a way that a maximum number of interesting and pleasant places may be visited, using the quietest and most attractive byways available.

The 'Main Circle Route' (Maps 1 – 12) shown on the Key Map opposite covers 130 miles and is far too long for a leisurely day's journey. We have therefore included three link routes (Maps 13, 14 and 15) which will enable you to make an 'East Circle Route', using Maps 1, 2, 3, 14 , 11 and 12; a 'West Circle Route', using Maps 5, 6, 7, 8, 9, 10 and 15; and an 'Inner Circle Route', using Maps 3, 14, 11, 12 and 13. At the same time you will note from the Key Map, that by using short stretches of various 'A' roads, it is very simple to make up your own shortened routes.

HOW TO USE YOUR BOOK ON THE ROUTE

Each double page makes up a complete picture of the country ahead of you. On the left you will find a one inch to the mile strip map, with the route marked by a series of dashes. Direction is always from top to bottom, so that the map may be looked at in conjunction with the 'Directions for the Driver', with which it is cross referenced by a letter itemising each junction point. This enables the driver to have exact guidance every time an opportunity for changing direction occurs, even if it is only 'Keep straight, not left!'

With mileage intervals shown the driver should even have warning when to expect those 'moments of decision', and if a signpost exists we have used this to help you with the 'Signposted.' column. However, re-signing programme is always in progress, and this may lead to slight differences in sign marking in some cases.

We have also included a description of the towns and villages through which you will pass, together with some photographs to illustrate the route.

To gain full enjoyment from your journeys be prepared to leave your car as often as possible. There are numerous small towns and villages to be visited, in addition to Constable's beloved East Bergholt, Flatford and Dedham, and the bustling towns of Colchester and Ipswich; and almost all of them justify exploration on foot. There are great houses like Audley End and Melford Hall, wildlife at Mole Hall and Stanway Hall, and fine churches like Thaxted, Kedington and Lavenham. In all but a few places, there is quiet contentment and an undisturbed rhythm of life, which you would do well to absorb. So drive slowly, stop often, and take time off to sample this tranquil watery landscape, with its willow bordered streams and woodlands, its splendid church towers and bright, cloud-scattered skies. The spirit of John Constable still lingers in this gentle countryside, and we hope that this guide will help you to discover some of its very special quality.

COMPILED BY PETER AND HELEN TITCHMARSH
PHOTOGRAPHY BY ALAN AND PETER TITCHMARSH

1

Map 1

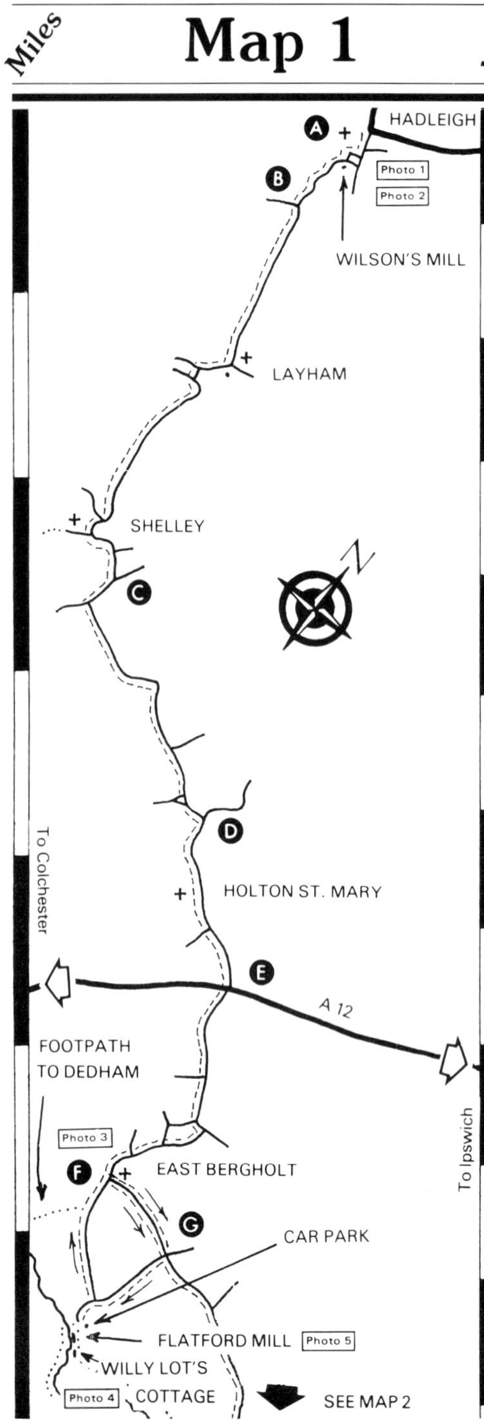

kms Ref. Miles	Directions	Sign-posted
A	Leave centre of Hadleigh on B 1070	Colchester
.1	Church up to right	
.1	Turn right off B 1070 [WATCH FOR THIS WITH CARE]	'U.R. Church'
.1	Bear left by the Ram Inn, and....	No sign
	Turn right by the Hadleigh Wine Cellars	No sign
.1	Over bridge crossing River Brett	
B .3	Bear left at Y junction	No sign
1.0	Layham church on left	
	Bear right immediately beyond church	Shelley
.1	Bear left	Shelley
.1	Turn left at end of village	Shelley
.9	River Brett on left. Attractive house on right, at entrance to Shelley	
.1	Straight, not right	Raydon
.1	Bear left (Road to church up to right), and... Over River Brett	No sign
.1	Fork right	Higham
C .2	Turn right at T junction	Higham
.2	Turn left at T junction	Holton St. Mary
1.1	Straight, not left	Holton St. Mary
.3	Bear left, and left again	East Bergholt
D .1	Turn right, on to B 1070	Ipswich
.5	Holton St. Mary church on right	
E .4	Straight, not left (But turn left if you wish to visit Ipswich... 9 miles)	East Bergholt
.1	Under tunnel beneath A12 Straight, not left	East Bergholt
.6	Straight, not right	No sign
.1	East Bergholt entry signed	
.1	Bear left just beyond the Beehive Inn	No sign
.1	Turn right by the Carriers' Arms	E. Bergholt St.
.2	Straight, not right	No sign
.2	Straight, not right	Flatford
.1	Post Office on right	
.1	Church on left, and....	
F	Bear left by War Memorial	Flatford
G1 .5	Turn right at X rds. beyond King's Head and... Into 'one-way' system	Flatford
.5	Arrive at car park for Flatford Mill, and.... TURNABOUT Bear left out of car park and into 'one-way' system	No sign
.6	Path to Dedham on left	
F2 .1	Turn right by War Memorial (Now re-tracing our steps)	No sign visible
G2 .5	Over X rds. beyond King's Head	Brantham
.4	Straight, not left, re-joining B 1070	Manningtree
	Total mileage on this map: 10.1	

CROWN COPYRIGHT RESERVED

On Route

Hadleigh
Busy little market town with a wealth of delightful buildings. Evidence of its prosperity as a wool centre in medieval times is to be found in the elegantly spired church, and the buildings which overlook its wide churchyard... notably the timber framed Guildhall and the mellow brick Deanery Gatehouse (1495).

Layham
The brick church tower looks out over the Brett valley and across the road to lovely old Netherbury Hall, with its handsome classical porch. The rather Victorianised interior of the church contains an interesting Purbeck marble font and an elegantly carved reredos dated 1905.

Shelley
Minute village beside the River Brett, with a small church which has a most pleasing interior. Here will be found late medieval panelling with a panelled pulpit to match, poppy headed chancel stalls, and a rather battered Elizabethan tomb.

Holton St. Mary
The stout, stumpy church tower is now topped with brick castellation, and the interior is darkened by its brown boarded ceiling.

Ipswich (See page 32)

East Bergholt
The painter, John Constable was born here in 1776, the son of a prosperous miller. His birthplace was demolished in the mid-19th century, and the cottage which he used as a studio is now incorporated in the garage beside the Post Office. However Constable's most enduring links with East Bergholt are the many pictures that he painted in and around the village, capturing for all time, the essence of the late 18th and early 19th century English landscape. He once wrote: "I love every stile and stump, and every lane in the village".

The church with its incomplete west tower, has a heavily Victorianised interior, but contains several items of interest. In the churchyard will be seen the graves of Constable's parents and that of mill-hand Willy Lot (see below). See also the unique 'Bell House', a 16th century wooden building in the churchyard, still housing the bells intended for the 'new' tower which was never completed.

Flatford
Flatford Mill, built in 1733, was owned by Constable's father, and added to by his brother in 1819. Willy Lot is reputed to have lived in the famous cottage bearing his name, just beyond the mill, for no fewer than 88 years. Both buildings feature in several of Constable's paintings. Walk from the car park which has picnic facilities, and having visited the National Trust's Bridge Cottage, with its information centre, shop, tea-room and boats for hire, cross the bridge to look at the handsome mill, or walk beside the River Stour to Dedham. Walk to the left of Bridge Cottage, passing the 'Granary Collection', with its interesting display of relics and bygones, to look at the outside of Willy Lot's Cottage. The mill is a Field Study Centre, and neither mill nor cottage is open to the public.

1. South Porch, Hadleigh   2. Near Hadleigh Church

3. At East Bergholt

4. Willy Lot's Cottage, Flatford

5. Flatford Mill

3

Map 2  Directions | Sign-posted

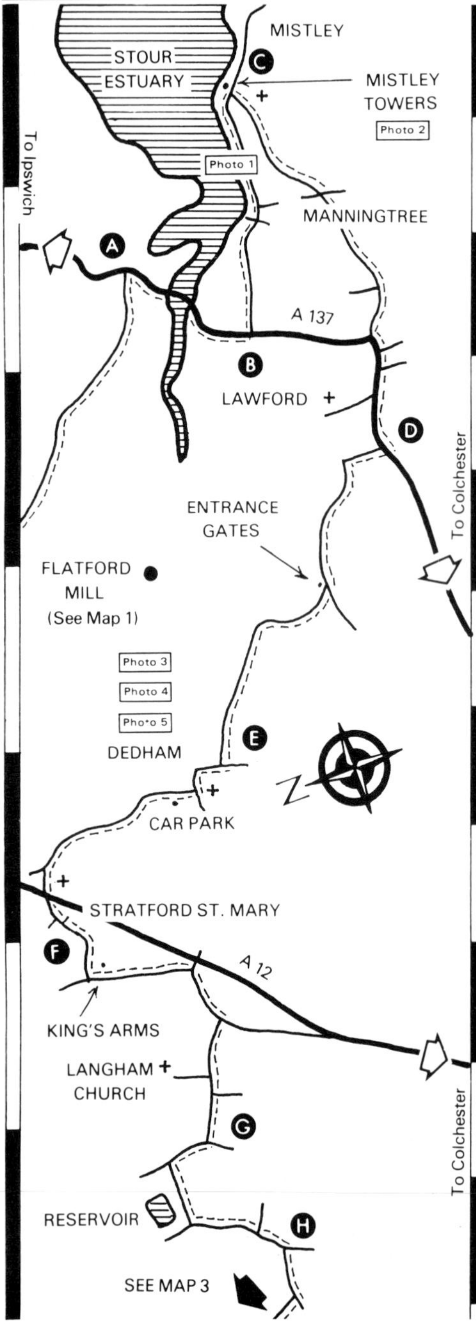

	kms Ref. Miles	Directions	Sign-posted
	.8	Brantham entry signed	
	.2	River Stour visible to right	
A	.4	Turn right on to A 137	Manningtree
	.3	Over Stour into Essex	
	.4	Under railway crossing, and...	
B	.1	Bear 1st left at roundabout on to B 1352	Manningtree
	.4	Manningtree entry signed	
	.2	Straight, not right	Manningtree
	.1	Over small X rds.	No sign
	.2	Stour estuary on left	
C	.5	Turn right by Mistley Towers on left	Colchester
	.2	Mistley church on left	
	.6	Over X rds.	Colchester
	.3	Lawford entry signed	
	.3	Straight, not right	No sign
	.2	Over off-set X rds., joining A137	Colchester
	.1	Straight, not left, keeping on A 137	Colchester
	.2	Straight, not left	No sign
	.1	Straight, not right, by War Mem. (But turn right if you wish to visit Lawford church)	No sign
D	.3	Turn right beyond King's Arms	Dedham
	.9	Fork right by second entrance gates	'Jupes Hill'
	1.1	Enter Dedham	
E	.2	Turn right at T junction (But turn left if you wish to visit Castle House.. .5)	Ipswich
	.3	Turn right at T junction, by church	Flatford
	.3	Riverside car park on left, and... over River Stour	
	.1	Suffolk entry signed	
	.8	Turn left, and.... (But go straight ahead, and then turn left, on to A 12, if you wish to visit Colchester... 8 miles) Stratford St. Mary church on left Under the A 12 road, and..	Stratford St. Mary
F	.1	Over off-set X rds.	Strat. St. Mary
	.5	Turn left by King's Arms River Stour on right	No sign
	.5	Le Talbooth Hotel and Rest. on right. Over Stour, into Essex	
	.1	Bear right up hill	No sign
	.4	Fork right, and... Langham entry signed	Boxted
	.3	Straight, not right by Lodge Cottage (But turn right to visit Langham Church... .2)	No sign
	.1	Straight, not left	Boxted
G	.2	Turn right at T junction opposite estate wall	No sign
	.2	Bear left at T junction	No sign
	.4	Turn left at T junction	No sign
	.4	Bear right at T junction	No sign
H	.2	Bear right at Y junction	Boxted
	.4	Boxted entry signed, and.. Fork left	Boxted
		Total mileage on this map: 13.2	

CROWN COPYRIGHT RESERVED

On Route

Manningtree and Mistley
Situated close to each other on the southern shore of the Stour estuary. Constable's father owned yards on the quay here and the barges that feature so often in the Stour paintings must have plied between here and the mills at Flatford and Dedham. There is still a pleasantly salty Georgian flavour about both places, and much of the shoreline is dominated by 'Mistley Towers', the only remains of Robert Adams' ecclesiastical work in England.

1. Low Tide at Manningtree

Lawford
In general this is a rather depressing place, but the church has an outstandingly interesting 14th century chancel with delightfully detailed stone carving, which should not be missed.

Dedham
Constable walked here each day from East Bergholt to the Grammar School. His father had by then purchased Dedham Mill, and in some ways Dedham seems almost as close to Constable, as his own village. However much of Dedham's charm is also derived from the prosperity of its clothiers, who built the splendid Perpendicular church in the early 16th century, and the handsome houses, shops and inns in the centuries that followed. Behind the church is a small 'Countryside Centre'. Castle House, which was the home of Sir Alfred Munnings, is also open to the public (see Route Directions). Dedham Mill, unlike Flatford, has been modernised out of recognition, but there is a car park overlooking the Stour, and 'skiffs and canoes' are available for hire.

2. Mistley Towers   3. Dedham Church

Stratford St. Mary
The church lies well outside the village, and has been over tidied by the Victorians. However there are two attractive little brasses and a lovely triptych reredos which should not be missed. In the village, another favourite of Constable's, there are several attractive timbered houses and inns lining the long single street but the once tranquil flavour of Constable's riverside is spoilt by a most unattractive pumping station.

Colchester
'Britain's oldest recorded town' makes an excellent base from which to explore the Constable Country. Space only allows us to mention—*The Norman Keep*, with its very interesting Museum...*The Abbey Gatehouse*...*St. Botolph's Priory Ruins*...*The Roman 'Balkerne Gateway'*...*The Minories Art Gallery*...*Holly Trees* (Social History Museum)...*All Saint's Church* (Natural History Museum)...and *The Zoo* in the grounds of Stanway Hall.

4. The Square at Dedham

Langham Church
This is quietly situated at the end of a long drive, and has a tower with brick castellation and pinnacles. The little building in the churchyard '*for the daily instruction of the poor girls of this parish*', was built in 1832. Do not miss the delightful '*Humble Petition for Dumb Animals*' in the porch.
Constable painted several of his famous pictures of Dedham Vale from Gun Hill, which lies between the church and Stratford St. Mary bridge.

5. Constable's River.... The Stour at Dedham

Map 3   kms Ref. Miles   Directions   Sign-posted

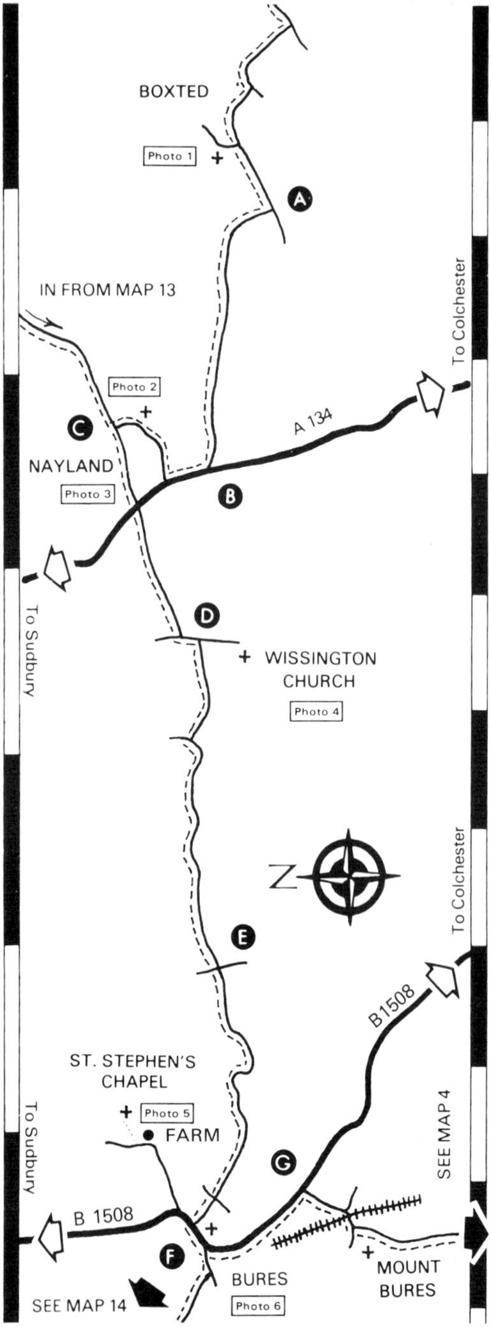

	kms	Miles	Directions	Sign-posted
		.2	Turn right at T junction	No sign
		.5	Turn right at T junction	Church St.
		.4	Straight, not right (but turn right if you wish to visit Boxted church. . . . 1)	Great Horkesley
A		.5	Turn right at T junction	Nayland
		.4	Views of Stoke-by-Nayland tower across Stour Valley	
B	1.1		Turn right, on to A 134	Sudbury
	.1		Straight, not left	Sudbury
	.1		Over bridge crossing Stour, and immediately.... Turn right	No sign
	.2		Suffolk entry signed, and.. Over second bridge at the entry to Nayland	
	.2		Church down to right	
	.1		Straight, not right (But walk down right to explore Fen Street)	
C	.1		Turn left at T junction WE ARE JOINED HERE FROM THE END OF MAP 13)	Colchester
	.4		Over off-set X rds. with great care, crossing the A 134 (Now following up the Stour Valley....river over to left)	Wissington
	.7		Bear left at T junction	Jayne Walker Hospital
D	.1		Turn right (But go straight ahead if you wish to visit Wissington church. . . .2)	Bures
	.6		Turn left at T junction	Bures
E	1.3		Over X rds.	Bures
	1.3		Over small X rds. at entrance to Bures	
	.3		Church on left, and... Turn left on to B 1508 (But turn right, and go straight, not left, up Cuckoo Hill, and walk down track past Fyshe House Farm, if you wish to visit St. Stephen's Chapel .8)	Colchester
	.1		Over Stour, back into Essex	
F	.1		Bear left, keeping on B 1508 (BUT TURN RIGHT NEAR THE SWAN INN FOLLOWING SIGN MARKED LAMARSH IF YOU WISH TO MOVE ON TO MAP 14, WHICH STARTS HERE)	Colchester
G	.7		Turn right at T junction, off B 1508	Mt. Bures
	.3		Straight, not left, just before level crossing	Wakes Colne
	.3		Straight, not right (But turn right if you wish to visit Mount Bures church)	No sign
	.4		The Thatcher's Arms on left	
			Total mileage on this map: 10.4	

CROWN COPYRIGHT RESERVED

6

On Route

Boxted
A scattered, very rural parish lying deep in luxurious orchard country. There are a few pleasant old houses close to the church. This has a whitewashed interior with its massive arcading and early 19th century west gallery well lit by clear glass windows, not least by those in the quaint little dormers.

Nayland
'LONDON 55 MILES' declares the handsome little obelisk mile-post at Nayland's centre, and there is no doubt that the prosperity of its clothiers allowed the import of at least a little of the capital's sophistication. . . .note the elegance of the mile-post itself, the 17th century curved hood over the door of nearby Alston Court, delightful little Fen Street with bridges over the mill stream, and the variety of pleasant houses and shops that abound. The church has a rather cold interior, but it has an elegant organ loft, fine roofs and clerestory, and a few surviving painted panels from a 16th century rood screen. Constable's painting of Christ over the altar is not one of our favourite examples of his work.

1. Boxted Tower and Dormers   *2. Fen Street, Nayland*

Wissington
Here at the end of a long 'cul-de-sac' road, beyond the site of a moated manor house, is a small Norman church with an apsidal (semi-circular) chancel. The Victorians may be forgiven for adding the pleasing little white painted bell-cote, but it is tragic that they found it necessary to 'Neo-Normanise' an already Norman building, with a variety of 'improvements' and furnishing. Fine chancel arch and sadly deteriorating wall paintings.

3. The Stour above Nayland Mill

Bures
The church lies close to a modest bridge over the Stour, and its Victorianised interior contains several items of interest, including the tomb chest of Sir William Waldegrave (1613) and his wife (1581), with kneeling children on its side. However the building of greatest interest at Bures is St. Stephen's Chapel, a small building in farmland well to the N.E. of the village (see Route Directions). A medieval foundation, it had been used as a barn until being restored in the 1930's. It now houses a splendid series of De Vere (Earls of Oxford) monuments, brought here from Colne Priory, and should not be missed. *Key available from cottage opposite (not always occupied), or Great Bevills or Little Bevills (both on Sudbury Road), or from Bures Vicarage.*

4. Wissington Church

Mount Bures
The Norman church, which lies to the immediate south of the earthworks of a Norman 'motte' (Hence Mount Bures), has a stumpy little shingle covered spire added in 1875.

5. St. Stephen's Chapel, near Bures   *6. Bures Church*

7

	Map 4		Directions	Sign-posted
		.1	Straight, not left	Chappel
		.4	Small chapel, and water tower on right	
	A	.2	Straight, not right at T junction	Chappel
		.4	Straight, not left at T junction	No sign
		.1	Bear left by pond	Chappel
		.4	Over old railway bridge	
		.2	Straight, not left	Colchester
		.2	Straight, not left at entry to Wakes Colne (But turn left if you wish to visit the East Anglian Railway Museum....1. See note opposite)	No sign
	B	.2	Over X rds. crossing A 604 (But turn right if you wish to visit Wakes Colne Church....4) (Note very long viaduct to left) Over River Colne into Chappel and pass the Swan Hotel	Great Tey
		.2	Chappel church down to right	
		.3	Bear left at T junction, keeping on wider road	No sign
		.1	Straight, not left at T junction	No sign
		.2	Straight, not left in Swan Street	'Swan Street'
		.2	Spendpenny Farm on left	
		.1	Straight not right by Pattock's Farm	No sign
		.2	Great Tey entry signed, and...	
	C		Straight, not right	Marks Tey
		.4	Straight, not left	Marks Tey
		.1	Turn right by church	'The Street'
		.2	Turn left at T junction	Coggeshall
		.6	Walcott's Hall Farm on right (not named)	
	D	.5	Bear right at T junction	Coggeshall
		.3	Buckler's Farm on right	
		.6	Bear left at T junction	Coggeshall
	E	.9	Turn left on to A 120	No sign
		.4	Turn right on to old main road	Kelvedon
		.2	And enter Coggeshall	
		.1	Over offset X rds. keeping on old main road	No sign
		.5	Road up towards church on right	
	F	.1	Turn left on to B 1024 (But go straight ahead for .2 to visit Paycocke's House, which is on left)	Kelvedon
		.1	Straight, not right, and over two small bridges crossing the River Blackwater	No sign
		.1	Track to left is right of way for pedestrians wishing to walk to Chapel, Mill, etc. (See opposite)	
			Coggeshall Grange Barn on right	
			Total mileage on this map: 8.6	

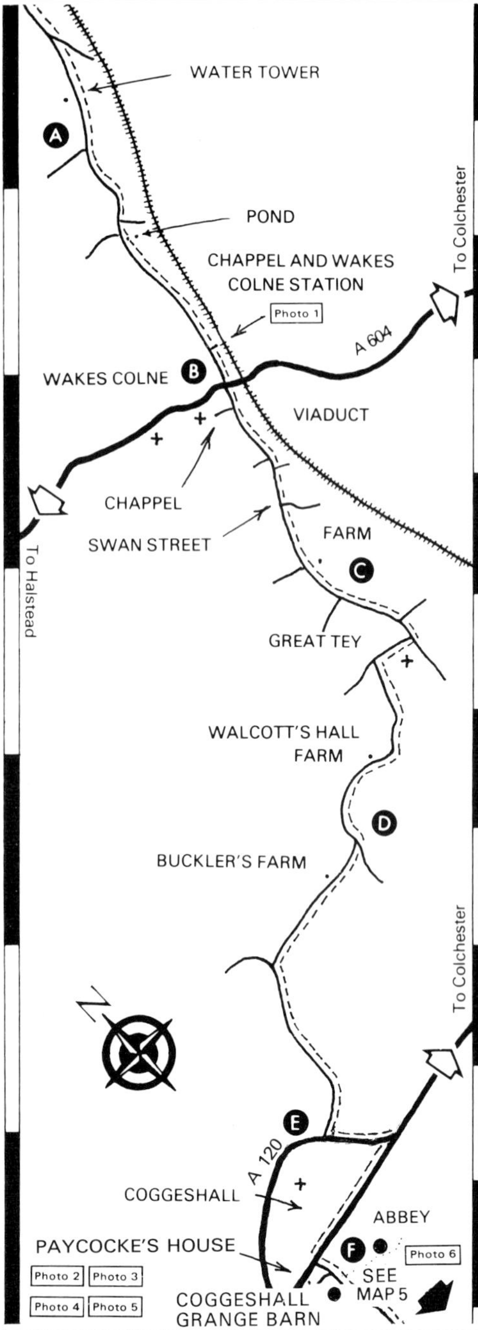

CROWN COPYRIGHT RESERVED

On Route

The East Anglian Railway Museum
Here can be found an extensive and interesting collection of locomotives and rolling stock.

Wakes Colne
The small Norman church has an attractive little weatherboarded belfry and the wall surrounding the east window are decorated with Victorian paintings... a rather appealing period piece

Chappel
Here is a small church with a slender little white painted spire, an old south door and a minute west balcony... everything on a small scale, and very pleasing. Not far away is a handsomely ornamented house, and beyond the church and farm there is a footpath leading close to a weatherboarded Georgian mill. A little to the east is a great railway viaduct spanning the Colne valley... over 1,000 feet long, and a fine piece of Victorian civil engineering.

Great Tey
An unexceptional village apart from its massively towered Norman church standing in a large open churchyard. This was originally a truly cruciform building, but the great nave was demolished in 1829 and replaced by a nave shorter than the surviving Norman chancel. The tower, with Roman brick much in evidence, is the finest feature, but although the interior is disappointing by comparison, the small west gallery, the Perpendicular font, the poppy-headed reading desk, and the mellow brick floors amply justify a visit here.

Great Coggeshall
This interesting little town has a church which was greatly damaged by a German bomb in 1940, but the subsequent restoration made a virtue of necessity, and its interior is now splendidly spacious and uncluttered. See especially the brasses of the rich clothier*Paycockes*, one of whom, Thomas, built 'Paycocke's House', a fine early 16th century timber framed house which is now in the care of the National Trust. This is an outstanding example of late medieval timber construction, and well worth visiting.

Little Coggeshall
Walk down the track (see Route Directions), past the Gate Chapel of St. Nicholas (now isolated in a field to the left, and remarkable for its brickwork, some of which must be 13th century... a very early example), then through a farmyard to a little bridge over the Blackwater. Downstream there is a delicious weatherboarded mill, and upstream a 16th century farmhouse incorporating the ruins of a Cistercian abbey (private)... a wonderfully atmospheric place, proving once again how adept the Cistercians were in their choice of sites.

Do not miss a visit to the National Trust's Coggeshall Grange Barn. Once part of the abbey and dating from about 1140, it is almost certainly the oldest surviving timber-framed barn in Europe.

1. Steam Loco at Chappel Station

2. Paycocke's House, Coggeshall

3. Door at Paycocke's House

4. Window at Paycocke's House

5. Carved Figure, Paycocke's House

6. Coggeshall Mill

Map 5   kms Ref Miles   Directions   Sign-posted

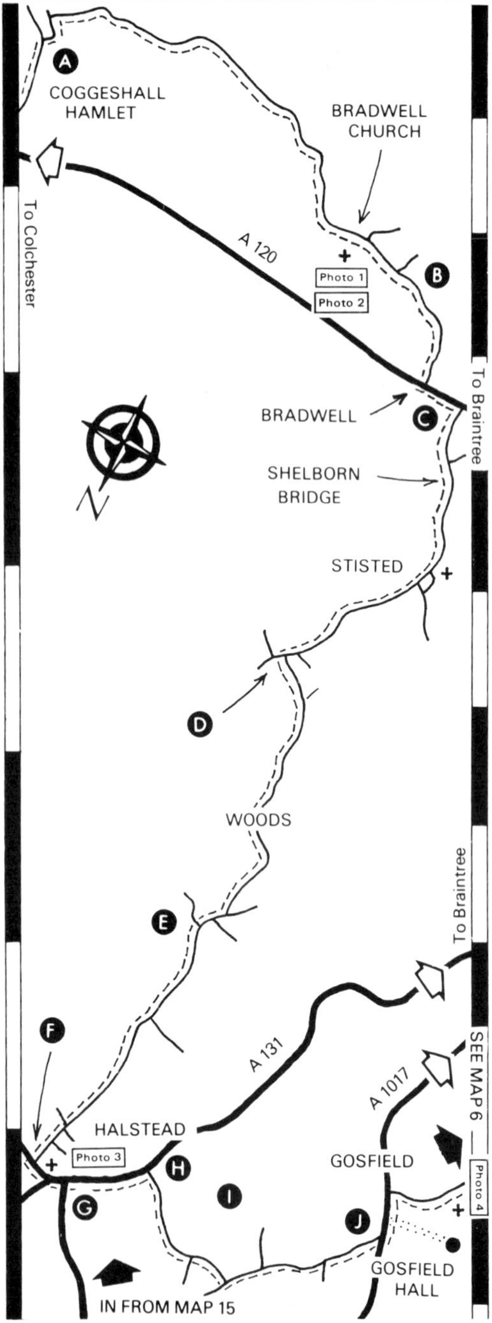

		Directions	Signposted
A	.4	Coggeshall Hamlet entry signed	
	.1	Turn right by house called 'The Hamlet'	No sign
	.2	Bear right at T junction	No sign
	2.4	Under electric power line	
	.3	Over small X rds. beyond wood (But turn down right to visit Bradwell church)	Braintree
B	.2	Straight, not left	No sign
	.5	Enter Bradwell village	
	.2	Bear round to right	No sign
	.1	Turn left on to A 120	No sign
C	.4	Turn right, off A 120 WITH GREAT CARE	Stisted
	.4	Straight, not left, and immediately... Over Shelborn Bridge crossing the Blackwater	No sign
	.5	Stisted entry signed	
	.1	Straight, not left (But turn left if you wish to visit church....1)	Greenstead Green
	.1	Straight, not left at end of village	No sign
	.8	Straight, not left, and....	No sign
D		Fork left by phone box	No sign
	.3	Bear right between two houses	No sign
	.8	Into pleasant woodlands	
	.7	Bear right at Y junction,	No sign
		Bear right at triangular green, and....	Greenstead Green
E	.1	Straight, not right at T junction just beyond	Halstead
	.7	Straight, not left	No sign
	.1	Enter Halstead	
	.5	Over small off-set X rds by Fire Station	'Parsonage St'
	.3	Straight, not left	No sign
F	.1	Turn left at off-set X rds	Colchester Rd.
	.1	Turn left by church, and almost immediately...	Chelmsford
G	.1	Straight over X rds (MAP 15 ENDS HERE) Down main street, and over bridge (River Colne)	Chelmsford
	.2	Bear right, keeping on A 131 by Bull Hotel	No sign
	.1	Bear left by Co-Op. House	No sign
		Straight, not right by garage	No sign
H	.2	Turn right by church (Keep straight out of town on this road)	Gosfield
	.5	Straight, not right	No sign
I	.4	Bear left, keeping on wider road	Gosfield
	.4	Straight, not left, keeping on wider road	No sign
	.7	Straight, not right	Chelmsford
J	.1	Bear left on to A 1017	Chelmsford
	.1	Straight not right (But turn right if you wish to visit Gosfield Hall....2)	No sign
	.1	Turn right by King's Head	'The Lake'
	.3	Gosfield church on right	
		Total mileage on this map: 13.6	

CROWN COPYRIGHT RESERVED

10

On Route

Bradwell-Juxta-Coggeshall

The village lies close to the A 120 and is not exceptional, but we come across the little church nearly a mile nearer Coggeshall, with only a tidy farm for company. Ask at the Rectory at Stisted (on our route well beyond point C) for the church key....a most temperamental piece of equipment which will require much patience... but once you have gained entry, all will have been worthwhile. There are two Jacobean monuments behind the altar, an interesting series of wall paintings, a 15th century rood screen, fragments of medieval glass, and a Norman font on an old brick pedestal. Do not miss this most appealing little church.

1. Monument behind the Altar, Bradwell

Stisted

Pleasant small village at the gates of 19th century Stisted Hall, with a church heavily restored by the Victorians, looking across a golf-course towards the River Blackwater. The shingled spire of the church was erected in 1844 when Charles Forster, grandfather of the novelist E. M. Forster, was rector here. We came across a herd of over fifty wild deer grazing over winter corn not far from the road, a mile or two beyond Stisted, at about the middle of the day. We hope you are equally fortunate.

2. Bradwell Church

Halstead

Near the head of the broad High Street stands the largely Victorian parish church, which contains an interesting series of monuments to members of the Bourchier family including Robert the 1st Lord Bourchier, who fought at Crecy and probably died of the plague. The High Street contains little of outstanding interest, but the white weatherboarded mill below the bridge, which was purchased by the Courtauld family as early as 1826, is still a very pleasant feature. The little gazebo-like building overlooking the mill pound was apparently a 'clocking-in' house.

3. Courtald's Mill, Halstead

Gosfield

The main village is just off our route and we shall confine ourselves to the church and to the Hall only. The church was built almost entirely of brick in the 15th and 16th centuries, with the addition of a handsome family chapel (now used as a vestry) in 1735. This has an elegant ceiling and contains a splendid monument to John Knight by the celebrated 18th century sculptor J. M. Rysbrack. There are also three interesting medieval tombs in the north aisle chapel. Gosfield Hall is a large Tudor mansion with a fine gallery of the same period and extensive later alterations. It is now owned by the Country Houses Association.

4. Gosfield Lake (See page 13)

Map 6

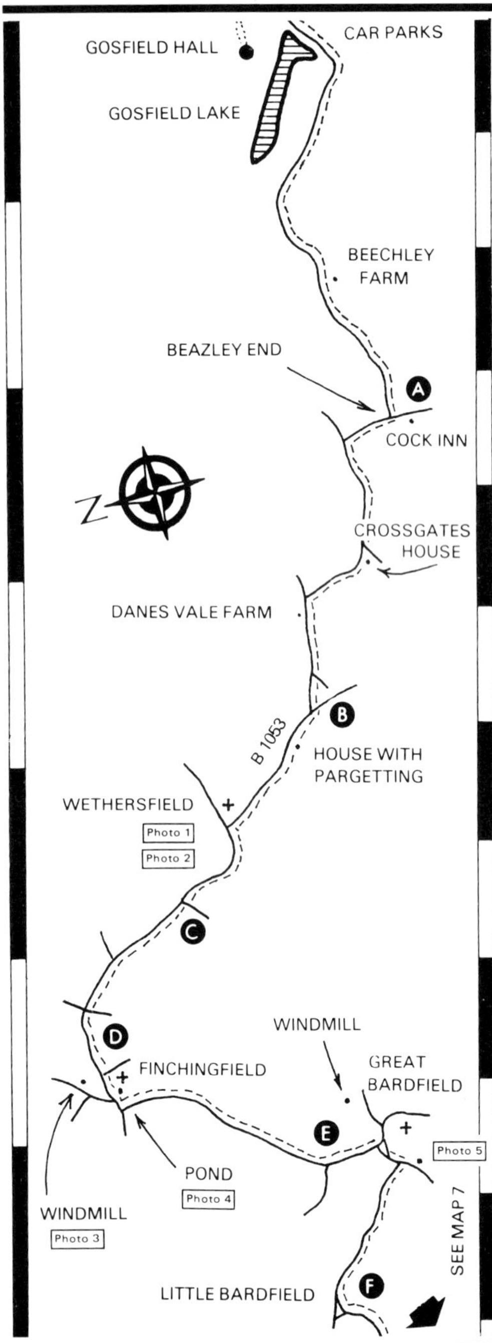

Directions — Sign-posted

kms Ref Miles		Directions	Sign-posted
	.2	Gosfield Lake on right (Car Parks just before on both sides of road)	
	1.6	Beechley Farm on left	
	.7	Farm with pool on left	
A	.2	Turn right at T junction in Beazley End (The Cock Inn down to left)	Blackmore End
	.4	Bear left at T junction	Rotten End
	.6	Straight, not left by Crossgates House	No sign
	.5	Bear left at T junction	No sign
	.2	Danes Vale Farm on right	
	.2	Straight, not left	Wethersfield
B	.3	Turn right, on to B 1053	Wethersfield
	.2	House with pargetting on left	
	.1	Wethersfield entry signed	
	.5	Turn left by village green (But turn right if you wish to visit church) (Keep out of Wethersfield on B 1053 as far as Finchingfield)	Finchingfield
C	.6	Straight, not left	No sign
	.3	Bear left at T junction keeping on B 1053	No sign
D	.4	Over off-set X rds.	No sign
	.3	Finchingfield entry signed	
	.5	Straight, not left by the Three Tuns	No sign
		Church on left Straight, not right, and...	Great Sampford
	.1	Over bridge by pond and...	
	.1	Bear left by War Memorial	Dunmow
	.9	Windmill visible over to left	
	.2	Great Bardfield entry signed	
E	.2	Straight, not right, and...	No sign
	.1	Over bridge, crossing River Pant	
	.2	Turn right at T junction (But go straight ahead and then turn left if you wish to visit church....3)	Dunmow
	.1	Turn right at T junction by timbered house (But go straight ahead for .1 if you wish to visit the Cottage Museum which is on the left)	Little Bardfield
	.6	Little Bardfield entry signed	
F	.2	Fork left by very attractive house dated 1602, with pargetted gables	Thaxted
	.1	Bear left at Y junction	No sign
		Total mileage on this map: 10.6	

CROWN COPYRIGHT RESERVED

12

On Route

Gosfield Lake
Gosfield Lake was created by Earl Nugent of Gosfield Hall in the 18th century and is a pleasant tree lined stretch of water on the edge of the park. In winter it is an excellent place for some quiet bird watching, but in summer it is given over to water skiing and boating, and there are facilities for camping and caravanning on the opposite side of the road.

Wethersfield
There are many pleasing houses and cottages in this rambling village centred upon its small sloping green sheltered by plane trees and overlooked by the Dog Inn. The church, with its stout stubby tower and smaller copper clad spire, stands near the head of the green....a delightful hotch-potch of flint and brick. The interior is unexceptional apart from the effigies of a 15th century knight (probably Henry Wentworth) and his lady, above which hangs a helmet with a unicorn.

1. Monument in Wethersfield Church

Finchingfield
Everywhere we look in Finchingfield, our eyes are filled with delight. Down the hill at our entry we see a wide green sloping gently down to a duck pond, itself overlooked by a 16th century inn and a variety of houses and cottages, all on varying levels. Arriving at the bottom, we see a white painted post-mill* over to our right, and then, having crossed the bridge by the Fox, we can look across the pond up to the hill we have just descended, to the 'Guildhall' (half almshouses, and half parish hall, with small museum), and the church tower with its attractive little cupola....surely one of the loveliest village prospects in all England.

2. Wethersfield Church   3. Windmill at Finchingfield

Explore Finchingfield quietly on foot....walk back up the hill, through a small passage-way beneath the 'Guildhall' to look at the church with its fine Norman west doorway and its sloping churchyard enriched by neatly clipped yews. The interior has shiny tiles and pitch-pine pews, but the Purbeck marble tomb chest with the brass effigies of John Berners and his wife (1532), and the 15th century rood screen, should certainly not be missed.

*Sadly lacking its sails when we called here last

4. Finchingfield

Great Bardfield
This is a special favourite of ours, with its wide streets overlooked by many handsome little houses and shops. We particularly like the Edwardian shop front to the Post Office stores and the elegant little Corniche Garage (Rolls Royce and Bentley distributors...no less). The church lies to the south west of the village, with a gold ball weathervane surmounting its spire, and a delightful chime to its clock. It is well known for its unusually massive chancel screen, although we felt this to be out of scale with its setting. Great Bardfield also possesses a brick tower windmill and interesting small thatched museum....the Bardfield Cottage Museum....with interesting exhibitions of Essex farming history.

5. Bardfield Cottage Museum

13

Map 7    Directions   Sign-posted

kms/Ref/Miles	Directions	Sign-posted
.3	Pleasant row of almshouses on right	
.2	Roadway to church down right	
	Entrance to Little Bardfield Hall on right	
1.9	Butcher's Arms and village green cricket field on left	
A .2	Straight, not right at T junction in Bardfield End Green (Not indicated)	No sign
.1	Straight, not right at Y junction	Thaxted
.3	Enter Thaxted	
.4	Turn right, on to B184	S. Walden
B .1	Straight, not left	S. Walden
.1	House on left... once the home of Gustav Holst	
.1	Guild Hall on left	
	Church up to left	
.1	Turn left immediately beyond church	Cutler's Green
.7	Cutler's Green entry signed	
.4	Through Cutler's Green	
.7	Turning to Woodhams Farm on right	
C .6	Over X rds. by electric power line	Debden
.2	Pleasant farmhouse to right	
.9	Debden entry signed	
.7	The Plough Inn on left	
.2	The White Hart on right, and...	
	Bear round to right by pond (But go straight ahead if you wish to visit church .1)	No sign
	Along pleasant tree lined road	
D .4	Over off-set X rds. (But turn left, fork left, through Widdington and then turn left at end of village if you wish to visit Mole Hall Wildlife Park... 3.3)	Saffron Walden
.9	Pleasant rolling, wooded country visible over to left	
	Total mileage on this map: 9.4	

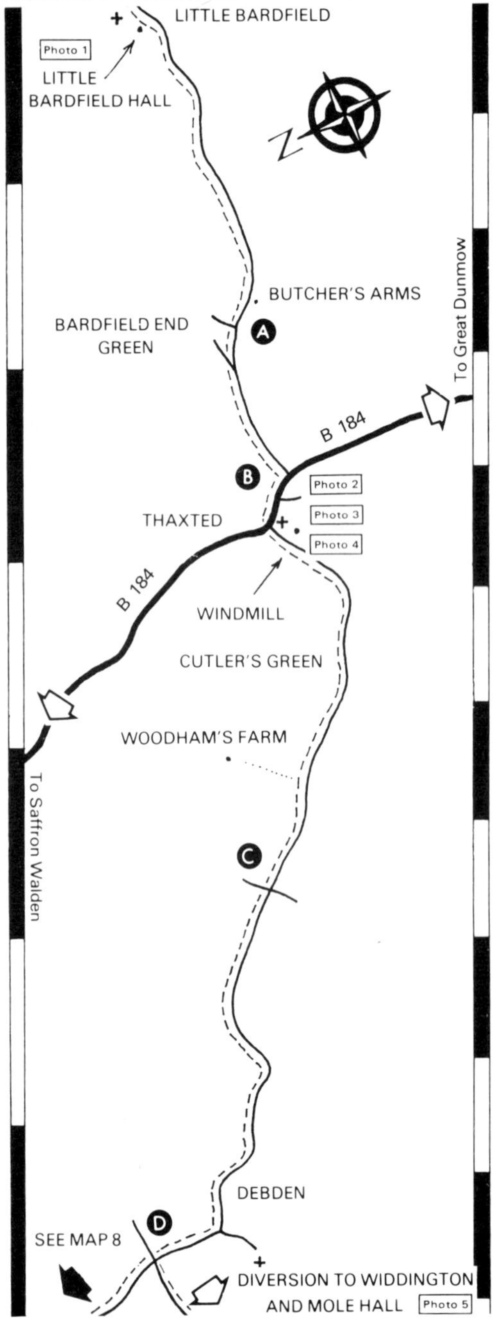

CROWN COPYRIGHT RESERVED

On Route

Little Bardfield
Quiet village with a pretty row of mellow brick almshouses (1774), an inn called the Spreadeagle, and a church with an Anglo-Saxon tower and 18th century organ (said to have come from Jesus College, Cambridge). Little Bardfield Hall, close to the church, has an attractive series of gables and extensive pargetting.

Bardfield End Green
Pleasant hamlet with a small inn, the Butcher's Arms, overlooking its wide green, and a few colourful farms and cottages.

1. Little Bardfield Hall   2. Thaxted Spire

Thaxted
This small town is a real winner. Approaching from the south-east as we do, our eyes are naturally drawn to the slender spire of its church, and then downwards, to the cobbled lane and the little timber framed Guildhall at its foot. This charming two storey building with over-sailing on both storeys, was built in the late 15th century, at a time when Thaxted's prosperity as a cutlery centre was at its height.

Climb the path to the church, which also reflects the wealth and piety of 14th and 15th century Thaxted. In our view this is one of the most satisfying churches on our route, with a finely proportioned interior, old stone floor uncluttered by pews, splendid old roofs, and light flooding in everywhere through mercifully clear glass. Having looked round this most interesting building, walk back down the main road from the north door, passing the handsomely fronted Clarence House, and explore the wealth of old houses, shops and inns, not forgetting a glance at Church Mill, a tall tower windmill, and second only to the spire, as a Thaxted landmark.

3. Clarence House, Thaxted

Debden
Situated in quiet farmland, Debden is a delightful village with a duck pond and hospitable pub, and many trees at its western end. The church lies well below the village, on the edge of an 18th century park with a tree bordered lake (the Hall, built by Henry Holland in 1796 was demolished in 1936). The church is largely the result of various Gothick essays on behalf of the Hall's owners, and is an unusually elegant little building with handsome detail....see especially the octagonal chancel, built like some miniature chapter house. Walk beyond the church to look at the lake from a small bridge....a tranquil bird haunted place.

4. Guildhall, Thaxted

Widdington
Pleasant little 'tucked away' village, centred upon a triangular green with a handsome Georgian rectory below its largely re-built church. Do not overlook the small brass to a civilian on a wall towards the rear of the church.

Mole Hall Wildlife Park
A large collection of animals and birds in enclosures centred upon an attractive and partly moated Elizabethan manor house. Don't miss a visit here.

5. Mole Hall Wildlife Park

Map 8

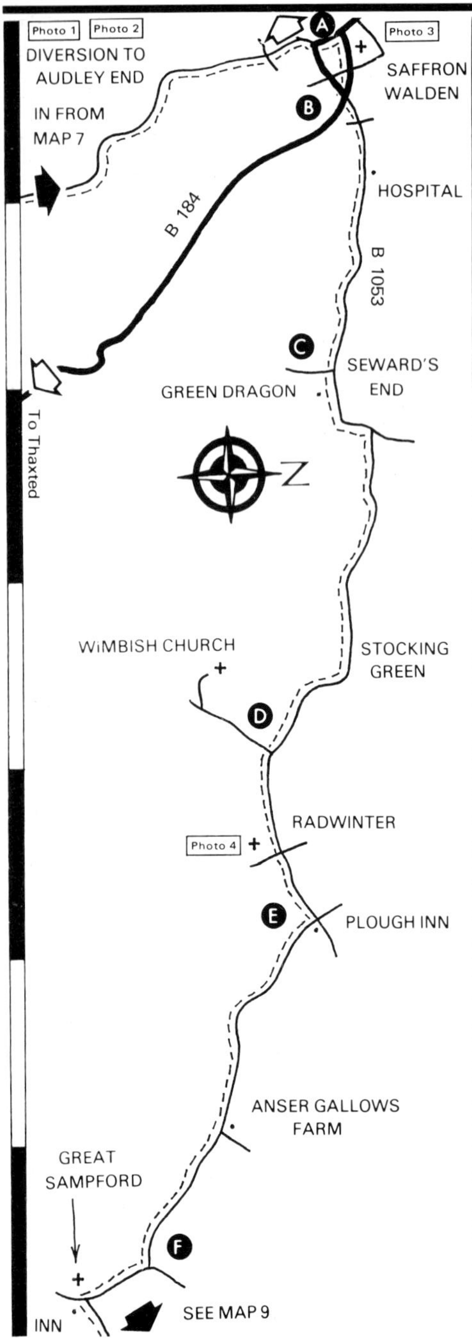

kms Ref. Miles	Directions	Sign-posted
.6	Pond and farmhouse over to right, in valley	
.7	Entering Saffron Walden	
.2	Over X rds. by the Crocus Inn (Keep heading into centre)	No sign
A .6	Turn right, on to B 1052, at the end of Debden Road (But turn left, and fork right twice if you wish to visit Audley End... 1 mile)	No sign
.2	Turn right in town centre, on to B 184 (But go straight ahead and take third turn to right up Castle Street, and then turn right again if you wish to visit church and museum....3)	Thaxted
	Over small X rds. just beyond	No sign
.1	Straight, not left	No sign
	Bear right	Thaxted
.2	Straight, not right, and...	Thaxted
B	Bear left, leaving the B 184 and joining B 1053	No sign
.1	Over small X rds. by gasworks	Sewards End
.4	Hospital entrance on left	
.7	Sewards End entry signed	
C .3	Straight, not right	Radwinter
.1	Green Dragon on right	
.4	Bear right, keeping on B 1053	Radwinter
1.4	Stocking Green down to left	
.1	Radwinter entry signed	
D .5	Straight, not right (But turn right if you wish to visit Wimbish Church..7)	Haverhill
.6	Radwinter church on right, and...	
	Over X rds. by the Red Lion	Haverhill
E .4	Turn right at X rds by the Plough Inn, keeping on B 1053	The Sampfords
1.4	Straight, not left, by Anser Gallows Farm	The Sampfords
.7	Great Sampford entry signed	
F .1	Straight, not left, keeping on B 1053	No sign
.4	Turn left at T junction by church, and the Black Bull Inn	Finchingfield
	Total mileage on this map: 10.2	

CROWN COPYRIGHT RESERVED

16

On Route

Audley End

We first encounter 'the village' on our left, with its charming little street lined on both sides with white painted cottages, and leading to 'St. Mark's College', 17th century almshouses which have been restored for the use of retired clergy. The mansion of Audley End is approached through the Lion Gate, a short distance beyond, on our right (also note Miniature Railway, almost opposite Gate).

Standing in a noble park, bordered by the River Cam, and landscaped by Capability Brown, with bridges, temples and an obelisk, Audley End is a magnificent Jacobean mansion (1603) with a wealth of fine furniture and pictures. Some idea of the size of the original house, the largest of its period, may be imagined when one learns that the present large building is only a relatively small fragment of the whole....the result of two phases of demolition in the 18th century. A visit here is well worthwhile.

1. Audley End

Saffron Walden

Saffron Walden, like Thaxted, was at the height of its prosperity in the 14th and 15th centuries (with the manufacture of cloth and the processing of the Saffron Crocus for dye, which was used for cooking and herbalism), but it is now about five times as large as Thaxted, and is a busy, bustling market town.

If possible park somewhere close to the church and explore the quieter part of the town from there. The slender spired church has a large, splendidly proportioned interior with fine roofs to the choir and nave, tall arcading and plenty of clear glass, but it does not have quite the appeal of Thaxted's church. Do not miss the excellent copy of Corregio's painting 'The Day' over the altar in the north chapel, nor the handsome monument to Lord Chancellor, Thomas Audley (1544) in black marble.

From the church, walk a few yards eastwards to visit the interesting small museum, and to look at the fragmentary ruins of the castle just beyond. Then walk down Market Hill, to the busy Market Place, to start a general exploration of this colourful little town, with its houses and inns, some pargetted, some with timber frames exposed, and many with over-sailing. See especially Myddelton Place at the beginning of Bridge Street; and the Old Sun Inn in Church Street, with its wonderful pargetting.

2. The Lion Gate, Audley End

3. Cottages below the Church, Saffron Walden

Wimbish Church....A Diversion

This is quietly sited close to a white weather-boarded house, and has a Norman south doorway, with a lovely old late medieval door. The interior is sadly Victorian in feeling, but there is a 15th century screen to the north chapel, and two most attractive small brasses to Sir John Wantone and his lady (1347).

Radwinter and Great Sampford (See page 19.)

4. South Porch, Radwinter

Map 9

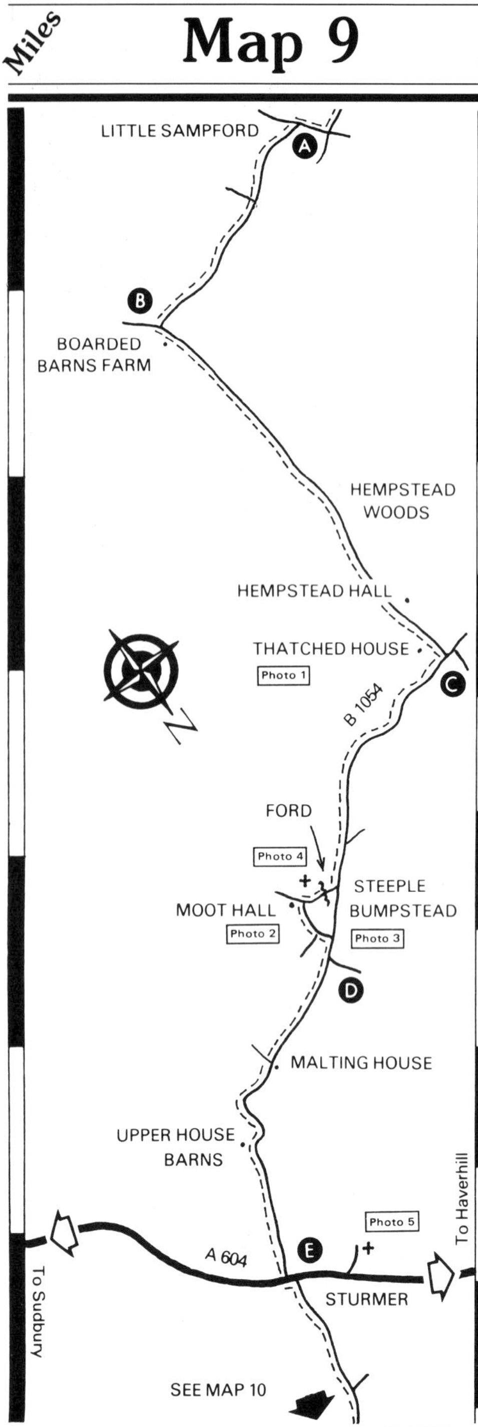

Ref.	kms/Miles	Directions	Sign-posted
	.2	Bear round to right by small X rds.	No sign
A	.2	Turn left by Little Sampford entry sign	Cornish Hall End
	.7	Straight, not right	No sign
B	.8	Turn left at T junction	The Bumpsteads
	.1	'Boarded Barns' Farm on right	
	1.3	Hempstead Wood on left. Pleasant views ahead	
	.5	Hempstead Hall to left (Antiques)	
	.4	Pleasant thatched timber frame house on right	
C	.1	Turn right at off-set X rds, on to B 1054	S. Bumpstead
	1.0	Steeple Bumpstead entry signed	
	.3	Bear right on to wider road	S. Bumpstead
	.2	Turn right, through ford (sometimes dry)	Finchingfield
	.2	Church on right. Turn left by the Moot Hall, on to B 1057	Haverhill
	.2	Bear left, over bridge, and...	Haverhill
	.1	Turn right, keeping on B 1057	Haverhill
D	.1	Straight, not left, leaving B 1057	'The Endway'
	.7	Bear left at T junction by Maltings Cottages	No sign
	.6	Bear left by Upper House barns	
	.4	Over old railway bridge with filled in cutting	
	.4	Sturmer entry signed	
E	.1	Turn left in Sturmer, on to A 604, and almost immediately...	No sign
		Turn right, on to B 1061 (But go straight ahead for .4, and then turn left, if you wish to visit Sturmer church....6 in total)	Kedington
	.6	Suffolk entry signed	
	.2	Straight, not left at T junction	Kedington
		Total mileage on this map: 9.4	

CROWN COPYRIGHT RESERVED

On Route

Radwinter (See page 16.)
William Harrison (1534 – 1593), one of England's early topographers, and a most astute observer of Elizabethan England, was rector here from 1559 until his death, and his rectory still stands, to the south of the churchyard. The church, and many of the houses and shops in the village, were re-built by the Victorian architect, Eden Nesbit, but he was thoughtful enough to spare us the fascinating 14th century timber framed church porch.

1. Farmhouse beyond Hempstead Woods *2. Moot Hall, Steeple Bumpstead*

Great Sampford (See page 16.)
Has several attractive thatched and colour washed houses centred upon the Black Bull Inn and the church opposite, but all is rather spoilt by a vast pylon to the immediate south. The church is a long building with a pleasant old door, but inside there are pitch-pine pews and more shiny tiles, both looking as if they will last for ever without mellowing. Do not overlook the 14th century font with its attractively shaped cover, nor the little man being bitten by a dragon, amongst the leaves on one of the arcade capitals.

3. The Red Lion, Steeple Bumpstead

Steeple Bumpstead
A warm friendly village with a small ford situated at the bottom of its quiet street, on the left of which is a Post Office stores and handsomely porched inn. Opposite the inn stands a large 11th century church with its Norman tower and chancel still intact. The top of the tower and the two aisles are in brick, and in the pleasant colour-washed interior, there is an extremely fine monument with the figure of Sir Henry Bendyshe (1717) reclining nonchalantly between two barley-sugar columns, with the figure of an infant beside him. Nearby there is also a monument depicting Sir John and Lady Bendyshe (1740) on a medallion upon which a cherub leans. Do not miss the unusually elegant Perpendicular font.

Beyond church and inn there is another small shop, and some cottages, and beyond them a minute Guildhall or Moot Hall, a smaller version of the one we have seen at Thaxted.

4. Monument in Steeple Bumpstead Church

Sturmer
A long village with small houses and colourful gardens strung out along the busy A 604. The church lies at the end of a pleasant tree lined drive . . . .a small Norman building with a brick built 16th century porch. The Norman doorway within the porch has grotesque heads and a tympanum, but all this has unfortunately been daubed with white paint. The simple interior has a double hammer-beam roof and there is a wall tablet to William Hicks, who was rector here for forty-four years, and who had been a midshipman aboard H.M.S. Conqueror at the battle of Trafalgar.

5. Sturmer Church

Map 10

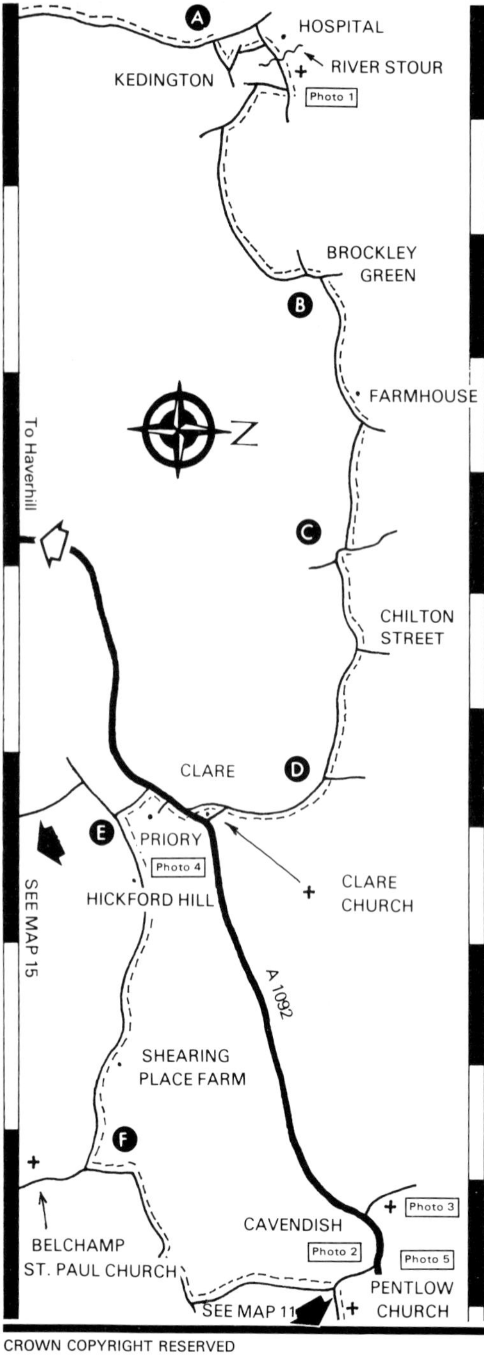

	kms Ref. Miles	Directions	Sign-posted
A	.9	Kedington entry signed	
	.1	Turn right at T junction	Hundon
	.1	Turn left at first T junction	Haverhill
	.1	Fork right by small doctor's surgery	No sign
	.2	Turn right at T junction by hospital entrance	No sign
	.1	Over River Stour by attractive mill house	
	.1	Church on left (DON'T MISS THIS)	
	.1	Turn right at T junction	Sturmer
	.2	Turn left by P.O. stores	Wixoe
	.3	Turn left at T junction	Hundon
B	1.2	Bear right at Brockley Green hamlet, and... Turn right beyond the Plough Inn	No sign Hundon
	.9	Bear right at T junction	Clare
C	.7	Bear right at T junction in valley, and...	Clare
	.1	Straight, not right	No sign
	.1	Stream now close to left	
	.4	Enter Chilton Street	
	.2	Straight, not left joining B1063 (Pleasant view up stream from bridge to our left)	Clare
	.6	Clare entry signed	
D	.1	Straight, not left, at Y junction, keeping on B1063	Clare
	.7	Bear right by church	'High St.'
	.2	Turn right by Post Office, on to A 1092	No sign
		Straight, not left (But turn down left to car park and pedestrian access to Clare Castle Country Park)	No sign
	.2	Turn left, off A 1092, and... Over River Stour, back into Essex	Ovington
E	.2	Turn left at T junction (BUT TURN RIGHT, FOLLOWING SIGN MARKED ASHEN, IF YOU WISH TO MOVE ON TO MAP 15, WHICH STARTS HERE)	Pentlow
	.8	Through Hickford Hill hamlet	
	.3	Transformer Station on right	
	.4	Shearing Place Farm on left (Note elegant bow front)	
F	.5	Turn left at T junction (But go straight ahead if you wish to visit Belchamp St. Paul church... .3)	Pentlow
	.3	Bear right at T junction	Pentlow
	.9	Pentlow entry signed	
	.1	Bear left at T junction by cottages	Cavendish
G	.8	Turn sharp right at T junction on to B 1064 and.... (But bear left and turn left, if you wish to visit Cavendish... .7. Do not miss this) Pentlow church down to left almost immediately	Foxearth
		Total mileage on this map: 11.9	

CROWN COPYRIGHT RESERVED

20

On Route

Kedington
A widespread village straddling the broad valley of the infant Stour, with a charming mill house and cottage situated just below the church. The long low exterior is tidy, but not exceptional, but once across the cobbled threshold of the south porch, and through the lovely medieval doorway, the extraordinary attractions of Kedington church become apparent. Here are mellow brick floors, quietly colour-washed walls, clear glass and fascinating furnishings everywhere. At the west end are 'children's benches' rising in tiers; there is panelling, box pews, a lovely three-decker pulpit, medieval benches, and a splendid collection of monuments. To visit here is to truly experience the England of the 17th and 18th centuries.

Chilton Street
An attractive streamside hamlet with a row of old cottages and the remains of an old mill.

Clare
Delightful small town with a fine Perpendicular style church surrounded on all sides by pleasant houses and small streets....see especially the pargetted 'Ancient House' (1473) and the attractively signed Swan Inn. The church has beautifully carved north and south doors which are contemporary with the Perpendicular rebuilding....unlike the lofty arcading within which is a survival from two hundred years earlier.

Clare Castle Country Park has an Information 'Centre' in an old engine shed and from here it is possible to visit the ruins of the castle's 13th century keep, and the delightful gardens of Clare Priory. This was the first Augustinian priory to be founded in England (1248) and it is good to report that the Augustinians were able to return here in 1953 after so long an exile. Some of the medieval remains are still visible, but please do not intrude beyond the gardens.

Belchamp St. Paul Church (See page 31.)

Cavendish
We first come across the lovely old mill house, set peacefully astride the Stour. And now down the ever busy main road to the duck pond and the village green, where Sue Ryder's Old Rectory* looks across to the classic Cavendish 'view', of tower and flushwork clerestory of the church rising above pink washed cottages.

*The Sue Ryder Museum, Shop, Tea Shop and Garden should not be missed. A visit here will help to support her invaluable work.

Pentlow Church
A small Norman building with a round tower. The unusual Norman font has an elaborate 15th century cover and the little north chapel contains a splendid early 17th century monument.

1. Monument in Kedington Church

2. Cavendish Mill

3. Church and Cottages, Cavendish

4. Archway, Clare Priory   5. Round Tower, Pentlow

Map 11 — Directions / Sign-posted

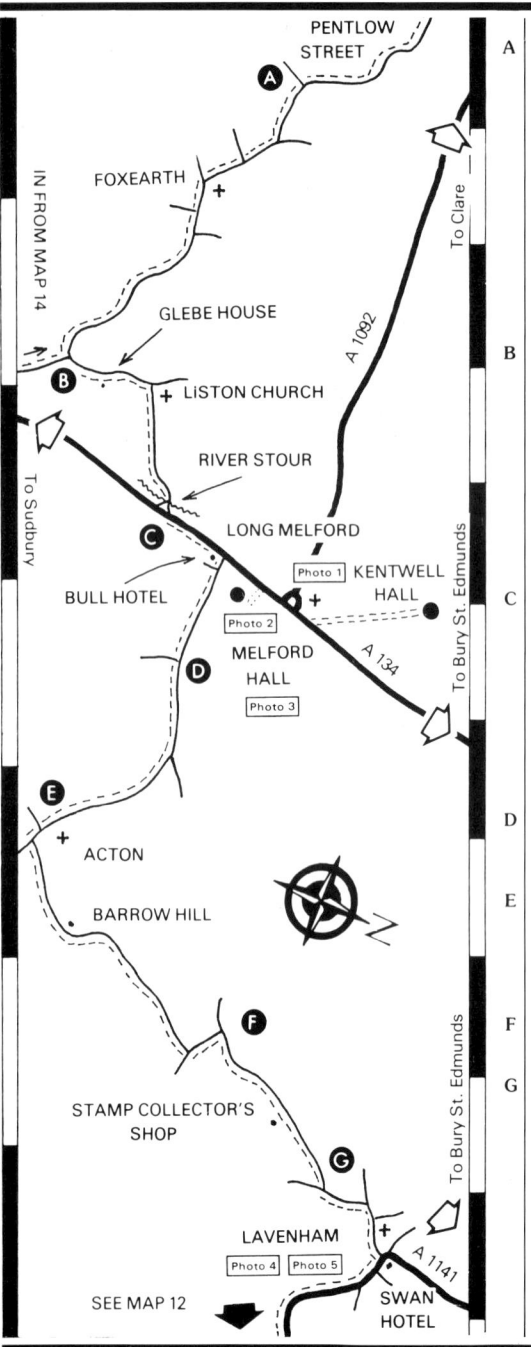

	kms Ref. Miles	Directions	Sign-posted
A	.7	Through Pentlow Street hamlet	
	.5	Bear left at Y junction, keeping on B 1064	Melford
	.3	Bear right, keeping on B 1064	No sign
	.2	Foxearth entry signed	
	.1	Straight, not right at T junction	Long Melford
		Moated farm on left just beyond junction	
	.2	Path down to church on left Bear left in village, keeping on B 1064	Sudbury
	.1	Straight, not right at T junction	Long Melford
	.2	Straight, not left, keeping on B 1064	Long Melford
B	1.0	Turn left at T junction, leaving B 1064 (WE ARE JOINED HERE FROM THE END OF MAP 14)	Liston
	.1	Liston entry signed	
	.1	Glebe House on right	
	.3	Turn right at T junction by Liston church	Long Melford
	.5	Over River Stour, into Suffolk	
	.1	Turn left at entrance to Long Melford, and... Immediately turn right	No sign / No sign
C	.2	Turn left, with care, on to A 134, into High Street	No sign
	.4	Turn right at T junction by the Bull Hotel, and almost immediately... (But go straight ahead to visit Melford Hall and/or Church... .5, and/or Kentwell Hall... 1.0)	Acton
		Straight, not right, just beyond the Bull	No sign
D	.6	Straight, not right	No sign
	.5	Bear right at T junction	Acton
	.8	Acton entry signed, and... Church up to left	
E	.1	Straight, not right by the Crown Inn	Waldingfield
	.1	Turn left beyond Post Office up Barrow Hill	No sign
	.4	Through Barrow Hill hamlet	
	1.1	Turn left at T junction	Lavenham
F	.2	Turn right at T junction, on to wider road	Lavenham
	.7	Entering Lavenham	
G	.5	Bear left, on to B 1071	Lavenham
	.2	Bear right, keeping on B 1071	Bury St. Edmunds
	.1	Church on left	
	.2	Turn right by the Swan Hotel, on to A 1141 (But stop to explore Lavenham on foot)	Brent Eleigh
	.1	Straight, not left, keeping on A 1141	No sign
	.2	Bear right, keeping on A 1141	Brent Eleigh
		Total mileage on this map: 10.8	

CROWN COPYRIGHT RESERVED

22

On Route

Foxearth
Despite its charming name, this is an unexceptional village with a largely Victorian church.

Liston Church
Has a dark brick Tudor tower and an interior with a sad memorial to the Thornhill family, who were massacred during the Indian Mutiny.

1. Long Melford Church   2. Gazebo at Melford Hall

Long Melford
One of our favourite small towns, Long Melford stretches for no less than three miles along the busy A 134, and was prosperous for centuries with profits from the wool and cloth trade. Its southern half is lined with a variety of pleasant houses, shops, inns and hotels... note especially 18th century Melford Place and the timber framed Bull Hotel. Once across the bridge, Melford's character changes. On the right there is the handsome 16th century Melford Hall in mellow brick, and at the head of the green opposite stands one of Suffolk's (and England's) finest parish churches. Space does not allow adequate description, but be sure not to miss the Clopton Chantry Chapel, the monument to Sir William Cordell (builder of Melford Hall) in the chancel, the little alabaster panel of the Adoration in the north aisle, nor the east Lady Chapel with its sumptuous roof beams. Just beyond the village on the A 134, is the entrance (on the left) to Kentwell Hall, another mellow brick 16th century mansion (built by the Cloptons), standing within a moat, at the end of a mile long avenue of lime trees.

3. Melford Hall

Acton
The church lies at the end of an attractive avenue of lime trees and has an extremely elegant interior. This provides a fine setting for one of the oldest and most beautiful brasses in England... that of Sir Robert de Bures... 1302... and also two other excellent brasses. In addition there is also a sumptuous monument to Robert Jennens (1725), A.D.C. to the Duke of Marlborough.

4. Misericord with Musicians, Lavenham

Lavenham
This must surely be one of England's most fascinating small towns. Prosperous since the 13th century with the wool trade and cloth manufacture, its merchants erected a bewilderingly beautiful series of timber framed buildings, and by a rare miracle these have largely survived without a major fire of the sort that destroyed so many of our medieval towns in a few hours. Moreover Lavenham lacked the prosperity of other towns in the 17th and 18th centuries and 'improvements' were fortunately rare.
The magnificently towered Perpendicular church is a building of more dramatic appeal than Long Melford's
continued on page 25

5. Lavenham Guildhall

23

Map 12   Directions   Sign-posted

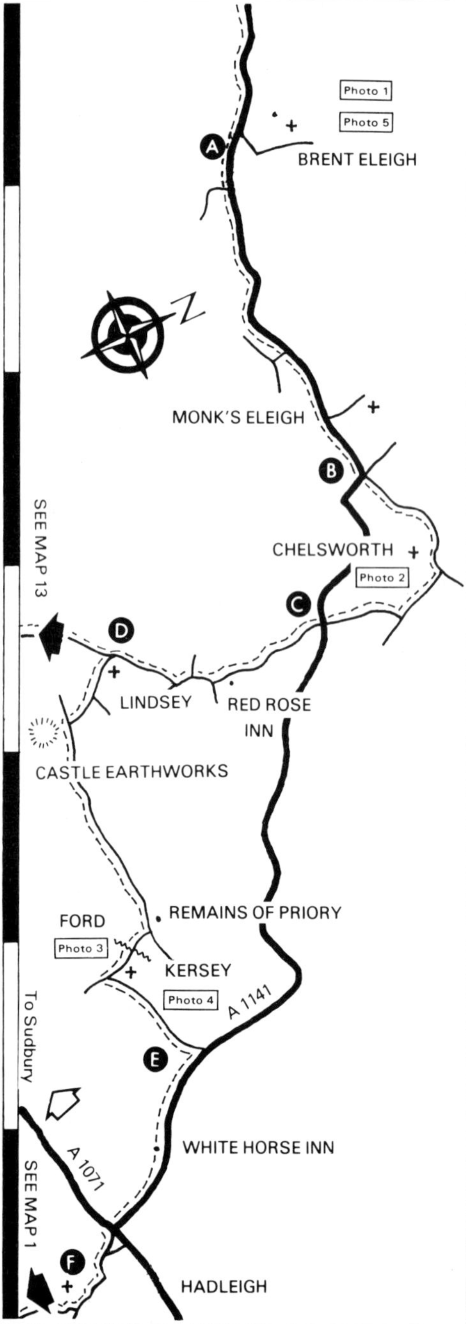

Miles	Ref	Directions	Sign-posted
1.4	A	Brent Eleigh entry signed	
.4		Straight, not left by the Cock Inn	No sign
		(But turn left if you wish to visit church . . . .3)	
.2		Straight, not right at end of village keeping on A 1141	No sign
1.1		Bear left, keeping on A 1141	Stowmarket
.2		Monk's Eleigh entry signed	
.2		Straight, not left by Swan Inn	No sign
		(But turn left if you wish to visit church . . . .1)	
.3	B	Bear slightly left at end of village, joining B 1115	Stowmarket
.4		Over bridge by Chelsworth entry sign	
.3		(Turn down right to church)	
.1		Turn right at T junction by Peacock Inn	Lindsey
		Over pleasant old mellow brick bridge	
.1		Entrance to Chelsworth Hall on right	
.3		Turn right at T junction	Lindsey
.4	C	Over X rds, crossing A 1141	Lindsey
.7		Enter Lindsey Tye Hamlet	
.1		Red Rose Inn on left	
		Straight, not left	No sign
		Straight, not right, and . . .	No sign
.1		Fork left	Boxford
.1		Fork right beyond Lindsey Tye	Boxford
.3		Enter Lindsey	
.1	D	Fork left by house called 'Monk's'	Kersey
		(BUT FORK RIGHT IF YOU WISH TO FOLLOW MAP 13, WHICH STARTS HERE)	
		Lindsey church on left	
.2		Straight, not left	Kersey
		Pleasant woodlands to right	
.2		Bear left at T junction	Kersey
1.2		Fragmentary ruins of Kersey Priory visible up drive to left (Private)	
.1		Turn right at entry to Kersey	No sign
.1		Through ford in village street	
.2		Church up to left	
.1		Bear left at T junction	Hadleigh
.8	E	Turn sharp right, on to A 1141	No sign
.1		Hadleigh entry signed	
.4		White Horse Inn on right	
.2		Turn left on to A 1071 and almost immediately . . .	Hadleigh
.1		Turn right on to B 1070	Hadleigh
.2		Now entering Hadleigh	
.2		Over bridge crossing River Brett	
.1		Bear right into High Street, and . . .	
	F	Arrive at centre of Hadleigh (LINKING WITH MAP 1, POINT A, BY GOING STRAIGHT OVER ON TO B 1070)	
		Total mileage on this map: 11.0	

CROWN COPYRIGHT RESERVED

On Route

Lavenham continued from page 23
church, but is not as exciting internally. However do not miss the misericords beneath the choir stalls, the chancel screen, or the nave and aisle roofs. Once in the town, park as soon as possible and explore on foot, making sure to include the Swan Hotel, the Wool Hall at its rear, the Tudor Shops opposite, the wide Market Place, with its cross overlooked by the Guildhall (National Trust....interesting displays), and the several streets dropping down from the Market Place.

Brent Eleigh

Small village with several pleasant houses, and an interesting church in a woodland setting close to handsome 18th century Brent Eleigh Hall. The church has a lovely early 14th century door heralding an interior containing several items of interest. The little building in the churchyard once housed a parish library, but this was dispersed many years ago.

Monk's Eleigh

The church stands well away from the main road, at the head of a small triangular green, complete with a charming old cast iron village pump (read inscription). Walk up the avenue of lime trees to the elegant south porch, and past the traceried medieval door, to visit the church's rather austere interior.

Chelsworth

Its street overlooks the little River Brett, which here flows through lush meadow land, past the church and finally beneath a two arched 18th century bridge. The very broad, short interior of the church is noted for its handsome 14th century tomb recess....a fine example of the Decorated style. The 'doom' wall paintings over the chancel arch were unfortunately over restored in the mid-19th century.

Lindsey

A scattered community in quiet rolling countryside with a modest church, whose tower was replaced in 1836 by a pleasing little wooden bell-cote. The colour-washed interior has box pews, a simple Jacobean pulpit, a handsome font, and well lettered 19th century boards.

Well to the south of the church (see Route Directions) there are the earthworks of a Norman castle. (For Lindsey Chapel, see page 27.)

Kersey

In late medieval times the Priory church (see Route Directions) must have looked down the steep village street, across the little ford, and up the other side to the splendid Perpendicular tower of the Parish church. Kersey was noted for its cloth (Shakespeare wrote of... 'russet yeas and honest Kersey Noes'), and no doubt water from the stream played its part in the processing thereof. So much of medieval Kersey remains, and it is a delight to the eye, with its timbered houses, many with oversailing upper storeys, lining the forded street, and all overlooked by the church. Although this has been much restored, the ceiling of the south porch, the nave roof, the painted panels from a 15th century rood screen, and the plasterwork in the north aisle chapel are all well worth seeing.

1. Brent Eleigh Hall

2. The Grange, Chelsworth

3. Ford at Kersey

4. Part of Rood Screen, Kersey

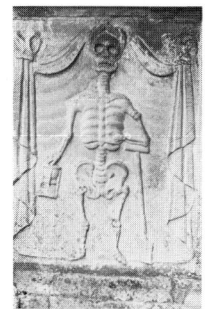
5. Father Time, Brent Eleigh Churchyard

Map 13  Directions | Sign-posted

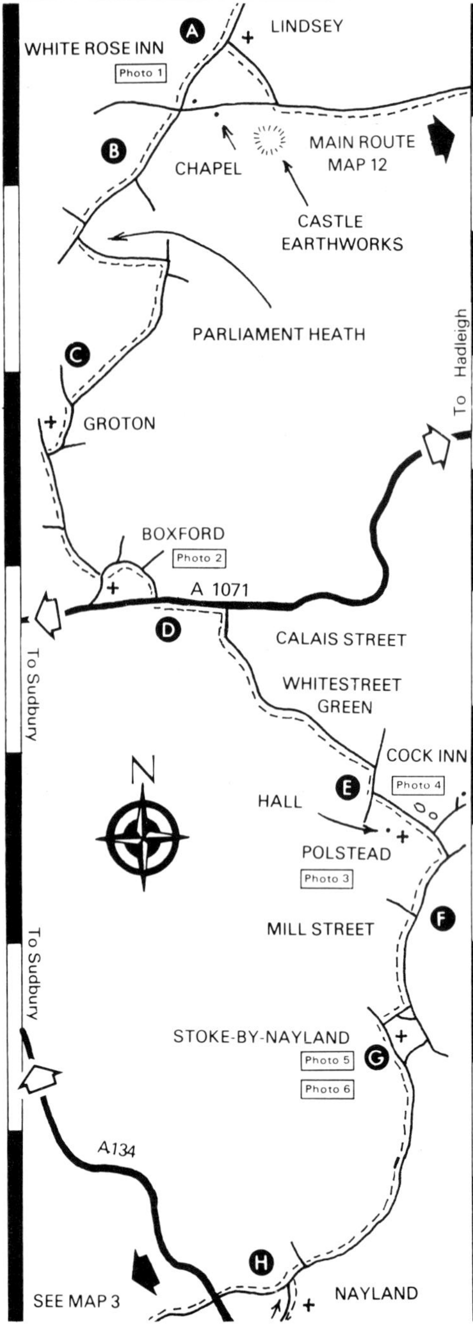

	kms	Directions	Sign-posted
A		Fork right at Lindsey, off Main Route, from MAP 12, POINT D	Groton
	.5	Over X rds. by the White Rose Inn (But turn left if you wish to visit the Lindsey Chapel)	Edwardstone
B	.5	Straight, not left	No sign
	.3	Straight, not right	No sign
	.1	Turn left at T junction by phone box in Parliament Heath hamlet	Kersey
	.6	Bear right at T junction, and...	No sign
	.1	Bear right at 2nd T junction	No sign
C	.9	Bear left at Y junction beyond Wainsway bungalow	No sign
	.1	Groton church on right	
	.1	Bear right at Y junction	No sign
	.1	Bear left by the Fox and Hounds Inn	Boxford
	.5	Straight, not right, at entrance to Boxford	Boxford
	.3	Turn left, on to main street, near church (Keep straight out of Boxford on this road)	Hadleigh
	.1	Straight, not left	No sign
	.2	Straight, not left at T junction	No sign
D	.2	Bear left, joining the A 1071	Ipswich
	.6	Turn right off A 1071 at Calais Street	Polstead
	.3	Over small X rds in Whitestead Green hamlet	Polstead
	.8	Turn right at T junction	Stoke
E	.1	Bear left at T junction	No sign
	.4	Enter Polstead. Ponds on left. Church up to right	
	.1	Straight, not left at T junction (But turn left if you wish to visit village)	Stoke
	.2	Turn right at T junction	Stoke
F	.4	Straight, not right, just beyond Mill Street hamlet	No sign
	.5	Turn right, and immediately... Bear right, at entry to Stoke-by-Nayland	Newton
	.2	Turn left at T junction	No sign
	.1	Church on left (After visiting church, walk through churchyard to explore village)	
G	.2	Bear right, joining B 1087	No sign
	1.1	Nayland entry signed	
	.3	Straight, not right	No sign
H	.1	Straight, not left, JOINING MAIN ROUTE AT MAP 3, POINT C	Colchester
		Total mileage on this map: 9.9	

CROWN COPYRIGHT RESERVED

On Route

Rose Green and Lindsey Chapel
This hamlet has an attractive thatched inn...the White Rose. Turn left here, if you wish to visit the Lindsey Chapel, a rather plain little medieval building, which was almost certainly built by one of the lords of the nearby castle (see Kersey, page 25). it was later owned by John Winthrop (see Groton, below).

Groton
Has an hospitable pink washed inn standing close to Elizabethan Groton Hall, which in its turn looks out directly over the churchyard. The church has a pleasant old tiled floor, a Jacobean pulpit, a battered 14th century alms chest and a fine old roof. The Victorian east window commemorates the first large Puritan emigration to New England in 1630, which was led by Groton's Lord of the Manor, John Winthrop. John founded the city of Boston and became the first Governor of Massachusetts, his son later becoming Governor of Connecticut. The town of Groton in Massachusetts was of course named after John Winthrop's village.

Boxford
The River Box is never far away, and the delightful village street is overlooked by woodlands acting as a backdrop to the church, with its handsome 14th century tower, topped by a little leaded spire. Do not miss the 14th century timbered north porch (one of the earliest timbered porches in the country), the handsome Perpendicular south porch in Caen stone, nor the font with its unusual cupboard-like cover.

Polstead
Up to our right, opposite two tree fringed pools, overlooked by a lovely Georgian farmhouse, there is a driveway to the church. This has a medieval stone spire looking across to Stoke-by-Nayland tower, and over its western churchyard wall to handsome Polstead Hall. In the churchyard there is a sign reminding us of the sad story of mole-catcher's daughter, Maria Marten, who met her much dramaticised end in the long vanished 'Red Barn'. The interior of the church has many interesting features including Norman arcading constructed of bricks (once believed to have been re-used Roman ones, but now thought to be some of the earliest examples of English brick-making).

Stoke-by-Nayland
Before visiting the church, do not overlook the two 16th century timber framed buildings opposite.... the Guildhall and the Maltings. However it will be hard to draw your eyes away from the dramatic 120 foot high Perpendicular church tower for long. This was a great favourite with Constable's and appears in several of his glorious landscape paintings.

Within the great vaulted south porch there is the lovely original door, with weathered and partly defaced figures in canopied niches....the very essence of late Medieval England. The noble interior *continued on page 29*

1. White Rose Inn, Rose Green

2. Porch at Boxford   3. Porch at Polstead

4. Pool at Polstead

5. Stoke-by-Nayland Church   6. Timber Framing at Stoke-by-Nayland

Map 14 — Directions — Signposted

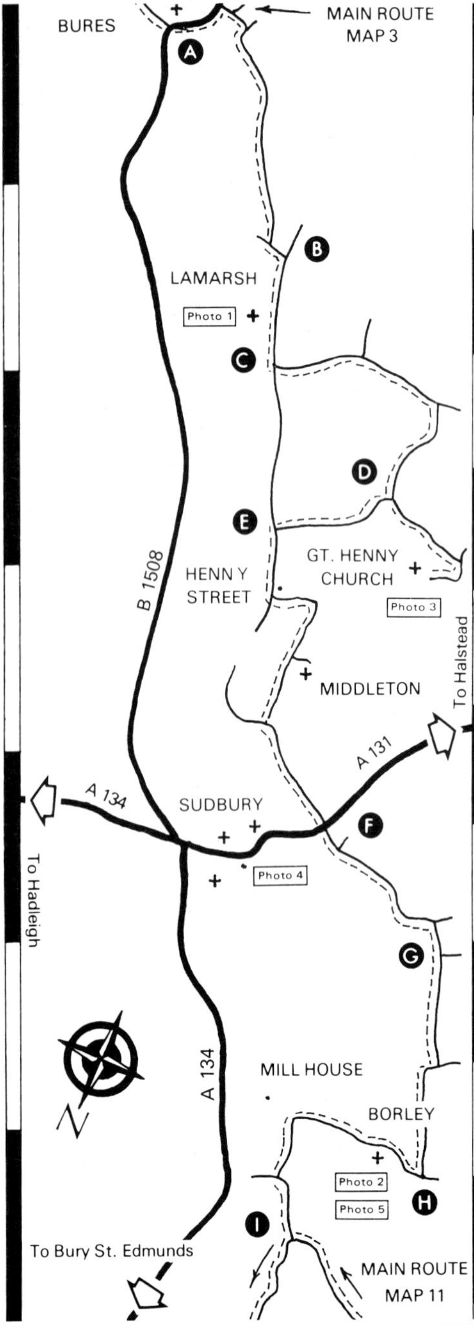

		Directions	Signposted
A		Turn right, OFF MAIN ROUTE, AT MAP 3, POINT F, near the Swan Inn beyond Bures Bridge	Lamarsh
	.1	Straight, not left, just beyond railway bridge	Lamarsh
	.6	Straight, not left	No sign
	.6	Pleasant views of Stour valley down to right	
	.1	Bear left at T junction Red Lion on left	Henny
	.1	Lamarsh entry signed	
B	.1	Bear right at T junction, and...	No sign
		Straight, not left	Sudbury
	.2	Lamarsh church on right	
C	.5	Turn left at T junction in wooded area Narrow sunken road with trees...drive with care	Twinstead
	.5	Straight, not left	Twinstead
	.5	Turn right at T junction	Great Henny
	.2	Attractive timbered house on right	
	.2	Through small ford	
D	.2	Turn right, and... (But turn left and then right, if you wish to visit Great Henny church.....9) Bear left almost immediately	Lamarsh
			No sign
E	.7	Turn left at T junction	Sudbury
	.4	Turn left at end of Henny Street hamlet	Middleton only
	.9	Middleton entry signed	
	.1	Turn right at T junction	Sudbury
	.1	Church up drive to left	
	.2	Bear left at T junction	Sudbury
	.3	Entering outskirts of Sudbury	
F	.4	Over X rds., crossing A 131, by King's Head **with great care**	Bulmer Road Industrial Estate
		(But turn right if you wish to visit Sudbury.....7)	
	.1	Straight, not left	No sign
	.8	Turn right at T junction	Borley
G	.2	Straight, not left	Borley
	.6	Turn right at T junction	Borley
H	.7	Turn right at X rds	Sudbury
	.3	Borley church on left	
	.5	Bear sharp left (Pleasant Mill House down to right)	No sign
	.3	Turn left at T junction, on to B 1064	Foxearth
I	.3	Fork right at Y junction (LINKING ON TO MAIN ROUTE AT MAP 11, POINT B)	Liston
		Total mileage on this map: 10.8	

CROWN COPYRIGHT RESERVED

On Route

Lamarsh
An unexceptional village on the edge of the Stour water meadows, having a Norman church topped by a delightful Rhineland Gothic style, conical tower.

Great Henny
A pleasant diversion through tranquil rolling country overlooking the Stour valley, takes us to Great Henny church. This has a Victorianised interior, but the miniature brasses of William Fyscher and his wife, and their fifteen children (1530) should not be missed.

Middleton
The small Norman church is situated below woodlands, up the drive to a Victorian house. The church has a plain Norman south doorway and a heavily restored Norman chancel arch. Do not miss the large painting of the Annunciation, attributed to the 'School of Veronese', and a most impressive piece of work.

Sudbury
Busy market town and light industrial centre, which makes relatively few concessions to tourism. However there are bright and cheerful shops, and in Gainsborough Street will be found the birthplace of fashionable 18th century painter, Thomas Gainsborough. This is a handsome Georgian town house, now partly a memorial to the artist, and partly an art centre, where regularly changing exhibitions are held. In the Market Place there is a fine statue of Gainsborough overlooked by St. Paul's church, which is now closed. St. Gregory's church, close to the Mill Hotel, is worth visiting for its splendid medieval font cover and its series of misericords.

Borley
The rectory here was for many years notoriously described as England's most haunted house, but it was burnt down in 1939, and all now seems peaceful hereabouts. Inside the church we found the fine tomb chest of Sir Edward Waldegrave (1561), with the effigies of the knight and his lady beneath a six poster canopy, the kneeling figure of one of his daughters on a separate wall monument, and a floor slab close to the altar to Humphrey Burrough (1757), a rector of Borley and an uncle of the painter Gainsborough.

Stoke-by-Nayland *(Continued from page 27)*
has, amongst many other items, splendid roofs, a soaring tower arch, a fine font, and a most interesting series of brasses, especially that of Lady Catherine Howard, great-grandmother of both Anne Boleyn and Katherine Howard.

Walk through the churchyard to explore the rest of the village, which is very pleasant, but has no items of exceptional interest. On leaving the village towards Nayland, spare a glance for the pools of Tendring Hall, the only survivors of the great estate owned by the Tendrings, and the Howards (Dukes of Norfolk).

1. Rhineland Gothic at Lamarsh
2. From Borley Porch

3. Farm at Great Henny

4. Gainsborough's House, Sudbury
Photograph provided by the Curator

5. Monument in Borley Church

Map 15

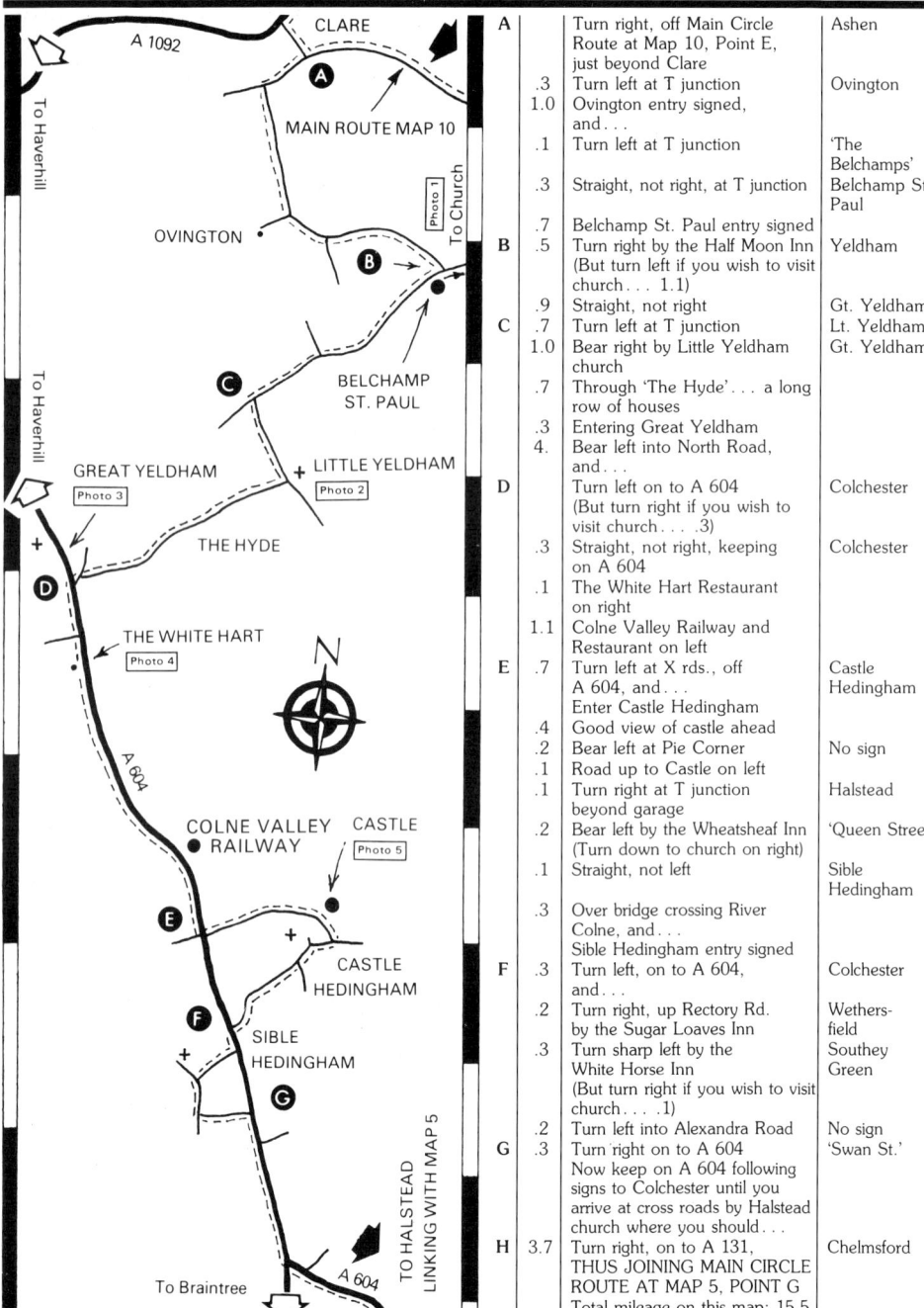

	kms Ref. Miles	Directions	Sign-posted
A		Turn right, off Main Circle Route at Map 10, Point E, just beyond Clare	Ashen
	.3	Turn left at T junction	Ovington
	1.0	Ovington entry signed, and...	
	.1	Turn left at T junction	'The Belchamps'
	.3	Straight, not right, at T junction	Belchamp St. Paul
	.7	Belchamp St. Paul entry signed	
B	.5	Turn right by the Half Moon Inn (But turn left if you wish to visit church... 1.1)	Yeldham
	.9	Straight, not right	Gt. Yeldham
C	.7	Turn left at T junction	Lt. Yeldham
	1.0	Bear right by Little Yeldham church	Gt. Yeldham
	.7	Through 'The Hyde'... a long row of houses	
	.3	Entering Great Yeldham	
	4.	Bear left into North Road, and...	
D		Turn left on to A 604 (But turn right if you wish to visit church....3)	Colchester
	.3	Straight, not right, keeping on A 604	Colchester
	.1	The White Hart Restaurant on right	
	1.1	Colne Valley Railway and Restaurant on left	
E	.7	Turn left at X rds., off A 604, and... Enter Castle Hedingham	Castle Hedingham
	.4	Good view of castle ahead	
	.2	Bear left at Pie Corner	No sign
	.1	Road up to Castle on left	
	.1	Turn right at T junction beyond garage	Halstead
	.2	Bear left by the Wheatsheaf Inn (Turn down to church on right)	'Queen Street'
	.1	Straight, not left	Sible Hedingham
	.3	Over bridge crossing River Colne, and... Sible Hedingham entry signed	
F	.3	Turn left, on to A 604, and...	Colchester
	.2	Turn right, up Rectory Rd. by the Sugar Loaves Inn	Wethersfield
	.3	Turn sharp left by the White Horse Inn (But turn right if you wish to visit church....1)	Southey Green
	.2	Turn left into Alexandra Road	No sign
G	.3	Turn right on to A 604 Now keep on A 604 following signs to Colchester until you arrive at cross roads by Halstead church where you should...	'Swan St.'
H	3.7	Turn right, on to A 131, THUS JOINING MAIN CIRCLE ROUTE AT MAP 5, POINT G Total mileage on this map: 15.5	Chelmsford

CROWN COPYRIGHT RESERVED

On Route

Belchamp St. Paul
Small village with a trim pub overlooking its wide green. The church, which once belonged to St. Paul's Cathedral, is situated in open countryside about a mile to the N.E., a pleasant building whose contents include two medieval misericords....the only ones in Essex, apart from those at Castle Hedingham (see below).

Little Yeldham
Minute village with small, over restored church overlooking a triangular green with trees. However this has a neat Perpendicular font and a 15th century belfry supported internally by massive oak posts.

Great Yeldham
Situated in the Colne valley, this village is unexceptional apart from its church, which has a Victorianised interior. However we liked the ogival south doorway, the medieval door, and the monument in the south aisle to Gregory Way (1799), with cherubs at is base.

Colne Valley Railway
Authentic railway buildings, track, rolling stock and locomotives, together with a restaurant car, book shop, souvenir shop and riverside picnic area. Don't miss a visit here.

Castle Hedingham
The Keep (1130 – 1140) on its high mound overlooking this little town, is the only surviving part of the De Vere's (Earls of Oxford) great castle.... their main residence until it was dismantled in 1592. It is however one of the finest surviving examples of a Norman tower keep in the country and well worth visiting. Descending into the town, one is immediately attracted by the diversity and charm of its buildings....from the timber framed Falcon Inn to the elegance of many a mellow brick Georgian town house and modest cottages of the 17th, 18th and 19th centuries.

Despite outward indications of 16th century origins, the interior of the church leaves no doubt that it must have been started at almost the same time as the castle. See especially the splendid north and south doorways, the arcading, the chancel arch, the deep set windows, and the charming misericords beneath the chancel stalls.

Sible Hedingham
With modern housing, factories and the ever busy A 604, this is all rather a shattering contrast to Castle Hedingham. The steeply sited church has been very much tidied up inside, but it contains a tomb chest in its south aisle, believed to be in memory of Sir John Hawkwood (1394), a mercenary who became general of the Florentine army, and who married the daughter of the Duke of Milan. His body lies in Florence, where there is a well known fresco of him by Uccello.

1. Belchamp St. Paul Church   2. Font at Little Yeldham

3. Cherubs at Great Yeldham

4. The White Hart, Great Yeldham   5. The Keep, Castle Hedingham

6. The Ancient House, Ipswich (see page 32)
A Jarrold Photograph

INDEX

	Page		Page		Page
Acton	23	Dedham Vale	5	Mistley	5
Adam, Robert	5	De Vere Family	7, 31	Mole Hall Wildlife Park	15
Ancient House	32	East Anglian Railway Museum	9	Monk's Eleigh	25
Audley End	17	East Bergholt	3	Mount Bures	7
Augustinians, The	21	Fen Street	7	Munnings, Sir Alfred	5
Balkerne Gateway	5	Finchingfield	13	Nayland	7
Bardfield Cottage Museum	13	Flatford Mill	3	Nesbit, Eden	19
Bardfield End Green	15	Forster, E. M.	11	New England	27
Bardfield, Great	13	Foxearth	23	Norfolk, Dukes of	29
Bardfield, Little	15	Gainsborough's Birthplace	29	Nugent, Earl	11
Barrow Hill	22	Gainsborough, Thomas	29	Oxford, Earls of	7, 31
Bendyshe Family	19	Gosfield	11	Parliament Heath	26
Belchamp St. Paul	20, 31	Gosfield Hall	11	Paycocke's House	9
Bergholt, East	3	Gosfield Lake	13	Pentlow Church	21
Blackwater, River	9, 11	Granary Collection, The	3	Pentlow Street	22
Boleyn, Anne	29	Great Bardfield	13	Polstead	27
Borley	29	Great Coggeshall	9	Puritans, The	27
Boston, Massachusetts	27	Great Henny	29	Radwinter	16, 19
Bourchier Family	11	Great Sampford	16, 19	Red Barn, The	27
Boxford	27	Great Tey	9	Rose Green	27
Box, River	27	Great Yeldham	31	Ryder, Miss Sue	21
Boxted	7	Groton	27	Rysbrack, J. M.	11
Bradwell-juxta-Coggeshall	11	Gronton, Massachusetts	27	Saffron Walden	17
Brent Eleigh	25	Gun Hill	5	St. Botolph's Priory	5
Brett, River	25	Hadleigh	3	St. Mark's College	17
Brett Valley	3	Halstead	11	St. Paul's Cathedral	31
Bridge Cottage, Flatford	3	Harrison, William	19	St. Stephen's Chapel	7
Brockley Green	20	Hawkwood, Sir John	31	Sampford, Little	18
Brown, Capability	17	Hempstead Wood	18	Sampford, Great	16, 19
Bull Hotel, Long Melford	23	Henny, Great	29	Sewards End	16
Bures	7	Henny Street	28	Shelborn Bridge	10
Calais Street	26	Hickford Hill	20	Shelley	3
Castle Hedingham	31	Holland, Henry	15	Sible Hedingham	31
Castle House, Dedham	5	Holly Trees, The	5	Steeple Bumpstead	19
Cavendish	21	Holton, St. Mary	3	Stisted	11
Chappel	9	Howard Family	29	Stoke-by-Nayland	27, 29
Chelsworth	25	Ipswich	32	Stour, River	3, 7
Chilton Street	21	Kedington	21	Stratford St. Mary	5
Christchurch Mansion	32	Kentwell Hall	23	Sturmer	19
Cistercians, The	9	Kersey	25	Sudbury	29
Clare	21	Lamarsh	29	Swan Hotel, Lavenham	25
Clare Castle & Country Park	21	Langham Church	5	Swan Street	8
Clare Priory	21	Lavenham	23, 25	Tendring Hall	29
Clopton Family	23	Layham	3	Tey, Great	9
Coggeshall Grange Barn	9	Lindsey	25	Thaxted	15
Coggeshall, Great	9	Lindsey Chapel	27	Thornhill Family	23
Coggeshall, Little	9	Lindsey Tye	24	Uccello	31
Colchester	5	Liston Church	23	Veronese, School of	29
Colne Priory	7	Little Bardfield	15	Wakes Colne	9
Colne Valley	9	Little Coggeshall	9	Wethersfield	13
Colne Valley Railway	31	Little Yeldham	31	White Street Green	26
Connecticut	27	Long Melford	23	Widdington	15
Constable, John	3, 5, 7	Lot, Willy	3	Willy Lot	3
Cordell Family	23	Manningtree	5	Willy Lot's Cottage	3
Corregio	17	Maria Marten	27	Wimbish Church	17
Countryside Centre, Dedham	5	Marlborough, Duke of	23	Winthrop, John	27
Courtauld Family	11	Massachusetts	27	Wissington	7
Cutler's Green	14	Melford Hall	23	Wool Hall, Lavenham	25
Debden	15	Middleton	29	Yeldham, Great	31
De Bures, Sir Robert	23	Mill Street	26	Yeldham, Little	31
Dedham	5	Minories Art Gallery	5	Zoo, Colchester	5

Ipswich (See Page 3)

Space does not allow us to do full justice to Suffolk's fine old county town, a major port with a population of over 100,000 people, and an excellent base from which to explore the area covered by this guide. However when visiting Ipswich do not miss: *The Ancient House* in Butter Market, with its pargetting and oriel windows (now a bookshop) (see illustration, page 31).

Christchurch Mansion, a splendid 16th, 17th and 18th century building in a large park, with an interesting collection of furniture and pictures (including works by Gainsborough, Constable and Munnings).

The Museum of Archaeology and Natural History in High Street, the contents of which include replicas of the splendid Sutton Hoo and Mildenhall Treasures.

32